PARLIAMENTARY SAUCE

Greg Knight, the Conservative Member of Parliament for Derby North, was born in the East Midlands and educated locally. Qualifying as a solicitor in 1972, he ran his own law practice for ten years, specializing in criminal law. He was elected to Parliament in June 1983. In December 1986 he was appointed Parliamentary Private Secretary to the Minister of State of the Foreign Office, becoming PPS to the Minister of Health in August 1988, a position he held until July 1989 when he was appointed an Assistant Government Whip. In July 1990 he was made a Lord Commissioner of the Treasury and in July 1993 he was appointed Deputy Chief Whip. He has written numerous articles for legal magazines and several comedy scripts for local radio. This is his third book.

His hobbies include music and the Arts.

PARLIAMENTARY SAUCE

More Helpings of Parliamentary Invective

Compiled by
GREG KNIGHT MP

Illustrated by
JOHN JENSEN

ARROW

Note: In the course of the production of this book there may well have been a number of changes in Members' positions in the Houses of Parliament. While every effort has been made to keep the text up to date, it may not have been possible where a change has taken place between the completion of the manuscript and publication.

Published by Arrow Books in 1994

1 3 5 7 9 10 8 6 4 2

First published in the United Kingdom in 1993 by Robson Books Ltd

Arrow Books Limited
20 Vauxhall Bridge Road, London SW1V 2SA

Random House Australia (Pty) Limited
20 Alfred Street, Milsons Point, Sydney,
New South Wales 2061, Australia

Random House New Zealand Limited
18 Poland Road, Glenfield
Auckland 10, New Zealand

Random House South Africa (Pty) Limited
PO Box 337, Bergvlei, South Africa

Random House UK Limited Reg. No. 954009

A CIP catalogue record for this book is available from the British Library

ISBN 0 09 943781 3

Printed and bound in Great Britain by
Cox & Wyman Ltd, Reading, Berks

For my brother Chris, in recognition of his helpful advice to me over the years, which I shall continue to ignore.

CONTENTS

ACKNOWLEDGEMENTS

The author wishes to thank the following for their help, advice, suggestions and assistance:

Rt Hon Michael Heseltine MP, Rt Hon David Mellor QC MP, Neil Hamilton MP, David Davis MP, Sir Nicholas Fairbairn QC MP, Rt Hon Alastair Goodlad MP, Peter Lloyd MP, Sydney Chapman MP, Andrew Mitchell MP, Jeremy Hanley MP, The Lord Waddington, The Lord Longford, Nicholas Bennett, James Moran, Renea Gummo, Janet Ormond and for her help with the manuscript, Teresa Sothcott.

The following books contain some excellent political stories, a few of which are recalled here and are acknowledged with grateful thanks:

Westminster Blues by Julian Critchley, published by Elm Tree Books, *F E Smith* by John Campbell, published by Jonathan Cape, *An American Life* by Ronald Reagan, published by Hutchinson, *Man of the House* by Tip O'Neill, published by Random House, *RAB The Life of R A Butler* by Anthony Howard, published by Jonathan Cape, *Baldwin, the Unexpected Prime Minister* by H Montgomery Hyde, published by Hart-Davis, MacGibbon, London, *The View from Number 11* by Nigel Lawson, published by Bantam Press.

INTRODUCTION

In the law there is a saying 'If you lose your temper, you lose your case.' Advocates in court are well aware that a cool head assists in the cogent presentation of an argument. It is a mistake to become rattled with one's opponent.

If all politicians were model lawyers, political debates would probably follow such a rule and speeches in Parliament would no doubt be more enlightening and persuasive.

But wouldn't it be dull? Many a serious debate is enlivened by a politician becoming irritated with an opponent or irked by a lack of attention from his audience. An explosion of temper may weaken a case, but it also brightens our democratic proceedings.

Bad temper, belligerence, bile and impudence are all part of the politician's armoury. Indeed, if a politician feels that his speech is not going down too well, he is likely to take time out to insult someone, not because he mistakenly thinks that the insult improves the oratory, but for a much simpler reason: it makes him feel better.

There is also another explanation for the frequency of the parliamentary insult. The 'audience' in either House is not exactly an impartial gathering, waiting to be convinced by the person holding forth. Unlike a jury in court, those listening *are* partial and do have a vested interest in the outcome. In the Commons, all MPs belong to a political party. Therefore, when a government minister rises to explain some policy initiative, by and large, the non-Conservative members are not waiting to be convinced. They are hoping for banana skins and blood. If a minister does well and handles the issues deftly, what is there left for an opposition member to do, other than insult him?

I am not suggesting that Parliament is failing in its duty. In Britain, both Houses do their job well. But, after several hours of debate, the mood of the House can only move in one of two directions: boredom or anger. When boredom sets in, who better than Labour MP Tony Banks to enliven the proceedings with an irreverent aside? If the insults are flying, who can top Tory MP Sir Nicholas Fairbairn for the crushing put-down? Even politicians known for their good nature (such as myself), have found that in debate there is a place for impudence and cheek.

Once, when I was confronted by a particularly pompous bore who boasted, 'Look here young man, I always speak my mind,' I could not resist the rejoinder, 'Yes, but unfortunately that limits the conversation.'

On another occasion, a newly elected back-bencher was bragging in the Members' Tea Room about how he was going to move an amendment in a Standing Committee due to sit later that morning. He explained that his amendment would be opposed by a Labour front-bench spokesman and added, 'It is going to be a real battle of wits.' I could not resist silencing him with the rejoinder, 'How brave of you to fight unarmed.'

I do not regret this or apologize for it – like the majority of my colleagues I accept that parliamentary insolence has its place. However, when insults fly, rational discussion and good order can sometimes be threatened. If an MP goes 'over the top' it is the duty of the Speaker to call him to order and require the withdrawal of any unparliamentary words used.

Because language and colloquial meaning change with the times, it is impossible to lay down hard and fast rules listing all the words or phrases which constitute unparliamentary expressions. Therefore, an insult may be in bad taste but within the rules of order. However, allegations of dishonesty by another MP or the use of obscene language *are* disorderly. But, because there is a grey area, most members of the House are expert in choosing a form of words which is highly offensive but is nevertheless in order. An MP can never call another a 'liar' but the House can be informed that a member is being 'economical with the truth'.

The most effective partliamentary insult is therefore achieved by hitting just *above* the belt. An over-the-top rant peppered with slander is likely to lead to the abuser himself being silenced. When the rulings of the Speaker are ignored she may 'name' the MP concerned. This a very ancient procedure where the MP is silenced by being thrown out of the chamber.

Severe as this punishment may sound, it is mild compared with what used to happen. On 2 March 1629 the Speaker rose to inform the House that King James I had ordered the proceedings to be adjourned. A number of MPs protested and this led to the principal speakers in the debate being arrested. They were all committed to prison, one of them being condemned to remain in the Tower of London for the rest of his life!

Over three hundred years later, have things really changed? Although these days the parliamentary punishment for being offensive is far more lenient, the invective remains as vitriolic as ever, proving that Niccolo Machiavelli was right when he remarked: 'Men pass from one ambition to another and, having first striven against ill-treatment, inflict it next upon others.'

Collected then between these covers are some of the most memorable barbs, insults and 'sauce' uttered over the years by politicians from both sides of the Atlantic. If some familiar names are absent this is for one of two reasons. Firstly, this collection is not a compendium of old chestnuts. I have tried to ensure that most well-worn and too-well-known quotes are excluded. Secondly, some prolific purveyors of acerbic abuse, such as Winston Churchill, have already been comprehensively covered by me in an earlier collection (*Honourable Insults*, published by Robson Books, 1990 – a book which, if I may immodestly say so, is well worth buying!). As before, I have tried to present an equal balance between the parties and not let my own views stand in the way of the inclusion of a good insult.

Finally, I wish to thank all of my relatives and friends for agreeing to see less of me during my work on this manuscript, a state of affairs that I hope will continue. And, to those people who profess to admire a man's wit but who view offensive and insulting behaviour with disdain, I commend the words of Aristotle. He accurately observed that wit, after all, is only 'educated insolence'.

Greg Knight MP
House of Commons
March 1993

1
Their Words Linger On

SIR ROBERT WALPOLE is widely acknowledged by historians to be Britain's first 'Prime Minister'. The description was not complimentary. The name referred to the accumulation of power and royal patronage in the hands of one single minister – something that was widely disliked and distrusted. A person so described was, in effect, the 'Sovereign's favourite'.

In an age when ambitious politicians often admit that they would like to be Prime Minister, it seems now rather strange that Walpole actually denied that he was a PM.

Although he was generally pleasant in manner, he frequently poked fun at his parliamentary colleagues. He carried on what was then the common practice of paying MPs for their votes, a habit which, in view of our current pay levels, has unfortunately fallen into disuse. After a 'pay-out' he was wont to remark: 'All men have their price.'

His speeches were generally blunt containing what would today be called 'plain common sense'. To colleagues who wanted to reform the system he would say: 'You will soon come off that and grow wiser.'

Many of his contemporaries regarded Walpole as a pacifist. Certainly he did not share the enthusiasm of others for the prospect of war. In 1739, on hearing church bells ringing to welcome a declaration of hostilities against Spain, he said: 'They now ring the bells but they will soon wring their hands.'

When he was asked why he had cultivated the friendship of Queen Caroline he replied: 'I took the right sow by the ear.'

Politicians who defended their actions by invoking patriotism, he silenced with the reply: 'A patriot? Patriots spring up like mushrooms – I could raise fifty of them within twenty-four hours. If I refuse to gratify an unreasonable or insolent demand, then up starts a patriot.'

He was popular but not universally liked. Jonathan Swift said of Walpole: 'He had some small smattering in books but no manner of politeness. The whole system of his ministry was corruption and he never gave a pension without telling the recipient what he expected from him, and threatening to put an end to his bounty if they failed to comply in every circumstance.'

Despite Swift's comments, most of Walpole's contemporaries spoke well of him and he was popular with the public. The nursery rhyme *Who Killed Cock Robin* is traditionally believed to refer to Walpole's fall.

Despite his protestations at being known as PM, the phrase stuck and the leading minister thereafter became known as 'Prime Minister' although no mention of the title can be found until 1878 when Disraeli signed the instrument of the Congress of Berlin as 'First Lord of the Treasury and Prime Minister'.

As the years passed, the post of the Prime – or first – Minister was usually held by whomsoever was 'first Lord of the Treasury' (today the British Prime Minister is also first Lord of the Treasury). The only exception to this rule appears to have been the first Earl of Chatham (William Pitt the Elder) who was never First Lord.

The power of the office of PM has grown substantially since Walpole's day. He was then actually more the monarch's spokesman in Parliament and his tenure of office was 'at the King's pleasure'.

LORD NORTH is regarded by many as the worst Prime Minister ever. His foreign policy was disastrous, but he did have some domestic successes. During debate he was very difficult to upset, using good nature and wit to great effect. On one occasion when he was addressing the House, a dog got into the chamber and punctuated every remark he made with a bark. This caused a good deal of amusement which nearly disrupted North's speech, but the dog was eventually removed. However, a few moments later, the animal found its way back into the chamber and began to bark again. North glanced at his canine interrupter and said, 'No, sir, you have spoken once already.' The House dissolved into laughter and his quip saved what until then had been a rather boring speech.

He frequently became bored himself! Once when it appeared that he had fallen asleep on the front bench, an opponent became enraged and shouted: 'Even in the midst of his perils the noble lord is asleep.' Without opening his eyes, North said: 'I wish to God I was.'

He said of the pressures of office, towards the end of his career: 'My anxiety of mind has deprived me of memory and understanding.' He went on to add, 'Capital punishment is preferable to that constant anguish of mind which I feel from running His Majesty's affairs.'

One of the critics of North's administration was the MP Temple Luttrell. When Luttrell sarcastically remarked that he hoped his contribution to the debate would not 'clog the activity of government', North brushed him aside with the riposte: 'No more than the fly which, landing on the wheels of a chariot, thinks that it has raised the dust with which it is surrounded.'

During a debate Charles Fox was speaking at length and was evidently filibustering to delay progress of the matter in hand. North turned on him and said that the speech reminded him of 'One of those maps by ancient geographers who concealed their lack of knowledge with pictures of elephants and other strange animals.'

According to one of his contemporaries, North was 'a course and heavy man, with a wide mouth, thick lips and puffy cheeks' – which seems a good description of his foreign policy.

Horace Walpole described him as someone with 'two large prominent eyes that rolled about to no purpose' (apparently he was short-sighted) 'and a deep untuneable voice. He had neither system nor principles nor shame.'

WILLIAM PITT THE YOUNGER, who became Prime Minister in December 1783, was the first to hold the office in a way that can be recognized today: he headed a cabinet of fellow ministers whose members he chose.

He entered Parliament at the age of 21 and by the time he was 24, he was Prime Minister – the youngest PM of all time. One of the reasons for his meteoric rise was that not only did he master the House of Commons but, in an age when the majority of the King's Ministers sat in the Lords, he was, for a time, the *only* government minister in the Commons!

To many colleagues he was cold and rather disdainful, frequently insulting friend and foe alike. Certainly, he saw little need to exercise restraint in invective. Within days of becoming an MP he confronted the then Prime Minister, Lord North, describing his policy on North America as 'accursed, wicked, barbarous, cruel, unnatural, unjust and diabolical'.

However, going over the top in invective was a dangerous pastime during Pitt's day. Once, when he impugned the patriotism of an Opposition MP, George Tierney, the back-bench MP challenged him to a duel – which Pitt accepted. Luckily neither was injured. The incident, although not intended as such, actually proved to be a good PR exercise: public support for Pitt increased dramatically afterwards.

When Pitt was criticized for his inexperience, he hit back with the riposte: 'Yes, I know I am young and inexperienced, but it is a fault I am remedying every day.'

WILLIAM COBBETT was a sharp-tongued radical politician who penned pamphlets under the pseudonym 'Peter Porcupine' which was very appropriate. Some of his opponents dubbed him 'a philistine' but most contemporaries conceded his vigorous and powerful campaigns against injustice.

He said of the revolutionary Thomas Paine: 'I do not know how he earns a living – or what brothel he inhabits – like Judas he will be remembered by posterity; men will learn to express all that is base, malignant, treacherous and unnatural by the single word – Paine.'

He also gave some good advice to political big spenders: 'Nothing is so well calculated to produce a death-like torpor in the country as an extended system of taxation and a great national debt.'

Cobbett died in 1835. Just after his death John Stuart Mill said of him: 'There were two sorts of people he could not endure. Those who differed from him and those who agreed with him. He always thought the latter stole his ideas.'

THE DUKE OF WELLINGTON, victorious at Waterloo, was one of the rudest men of his day. He was Prime Minister for nearly three years from January 1828 to November 1830, returning for a mere three weeks in 1834.

He was a reactionary who did not suffer fools at all and who usually spoke his mind. The problem was that he was completely out of touch with ordinary people and had no knowledge whatsoever of trade or industry. At the time of his death in 1852 a number of his insults had already become legend.

He said of Robert Peel: 'I may have no small talk, but Peel has no manners.'

The Duke heaped scorn on the cavalry, saying of them: 'The only thing that they can be relied on to do is to gallop too far and too fast.'

And in a similar vein: 'There is nothing on earth so stupid as a gallant officer.'

He was opposed to anything that smacked of a new idea and hated what he called 'modern music'. Once when he attended a performance of Beethoven's *The Battle of Vitoria* he was asked by a fellow guest whether the music resembled the real battle. He snapped back, 'By God no. If it had, I should have run away myself.'

Of the Prince Regent, later to become King George IV, he said: 'He speaks and swears like old Falstaff – I am ashamed to walk into a room with him.'

Asked what he thought of government minister William Huskisson, he remarked: 'He is a very good bridge for rats to run over.'

When, at a reception, two French marshals still smarting over their battlefield defeat turned their backs on him, he remarked loudly to an aide, 'It doesn't bother me – I have seen their backs before.'

Commenting on troops sent to him in Spain in 1809 he made the now famous remark: 'I don't know what effect these men will have upon the enemy, but by God they terrify me.'

Later, in a similar vein, he added: 'We have in the service the scum of the earth as common soldiers.'

On being asked by Queen Victoria the best way of removing hundreds of small birds from the new Crystal Palace, Wellington tartily retorted: 'Try sparrow hawks ma'am.'

After an election, watching the arrival at Westminster of new members of the House of Commons, he said: 'I never saw so many shocking bad hats in all my life.'

DIARIST DOCTOR SAMUEL JOHNSON took a keen interest in the politics of his day. He had a low opinion of Lord North, of whom he said contemptuously: 'He fills a chair.'

Of a colleague who boasted of his patriotism, Johnson

echoed the words of Walpole: 'Patriotism is the last refuge of a scoundrel.'

Commenting on a pension: 'In England it is generally understood to mean pay given to a state hireling for treason to his country.'

He had no time for angling which he defined as: 'A stick and a piece of string with a worm at one end and a fool at the other.'

Once when a conceited man was attending a dinner party he asked Johnson: 'Tell me, Doctor, what would you give to be as young and sprightly as I am?' Johnson immediately replied, 'I would almost be content to be as foolish and conceited.'

When the debate turned to the question of Ireland, he remarked: 'The Irish are a fair people: they never speak well of one another.'

Of a contemporary colleague: 'He was dull in company, dull at home, dull everywhere. He was dull in a new way, and that made many people think him great.'

On one's opponents: 'Treating your adversary with respect is giving him an advantage to which he is not entitled.'

On strangers: 'We are inclined to believe those whom we do not know, because they have never deceived us.'

Commenting on his fellow countrymen: 'When two Englishmen meet, their first talk is of the weather.'

To a fellow writer he gave the withering reply: 'Your manuscript is both good and original: but the part that is good is not original, and the part that is original is not good.'

Always a *bon viveur*, before his death in 1784 he summed up his own attitude to life with the quip: 'Whoever thinks of going to bed before 12 o'clock is a scoundrel.'

WHEN EDMUND BURKE addressed the Commons his speeches were so boring there was usually a mass exodus of members.

On one occasion when he rose to his feet, as usual the House quickly emptied. Seeing a large number of his colleagues leaving the chamber, a newly elected member inquired: 'Is the House up?' To which George Selwyn MP replied: 'No, but Burke is.'

He developed such a reputation as a boring speaker that it soon became popular for MPs to take refreshment – whatever the hour – when Burke rose to his feet. This led to his opponents giving him the nickname 'the Dinner Bell'.

THE CONSERVATIVE raconteur Reverend Sydney Smith coined a neat description of marriage: 'It resembles a pair of shears, so joined that they cannot be separated; often moving in opposite directions, yet always punishing anyone who comes between them.'

Known for his quick wit and barbed insults, when he saw Brighton pavilion for the first time he remarked: 'I thought that St Paul's Cathedral had come down and pooped.'

Of a colleague he commented: 'I like him and his wife. He is so ladylike, and she is such a perfect gentleman.'

He accurately perceived the lack of a sense of humour in many of our neighbours north of the border, mischievously referring to 'the incapacity of the Scots to take a joke without a surgical operation.'

On visiting the East, he was withering: 'The departure of the Wise Men seems to have been on a more extensive scale than is generally supposed for no one of that description seems to have been left behind.'

During a stay in London he saw Lord Brougham in his carriage and noticed a large letter 'B' surrounded by a coronet engraved on the door. When asked by a friend what he was looking at, he replied: 'I was gazing at that carriage. It has a B outside and a wasp within.'

Shortly before his death in 1845, he attended a performance

of Handel's *Messiah*. During the concert, he noticed Lord Brougham arriving late and observed loudly: 'Here comes counsel for the other side.'

BENJAMIN DISRAELI first entered Parliament in 1837. Between that date and his death in 1881 he displayed a remarkable talent for political oratory and insult.

Silencing Sir Charles Wood he said: 'He must learn that petulance is not sarcasm and insolence is not invective.'

Of the Earl of Derby he said: 'I do not know that there is anything which excites enthusiasm in him, except when he contemplates the surrender of some national policy.' Some MPs feel that, over the years, this remark could equally be applied to the British Foreign Office!

After he had faced a number of insults thrown across the chamber, Disraeli dismissed the criticism with the quip: 'A majority is the best repartee.'

Of two of his Commons colleagues for whom he had no respect: 'Their table talk is stable talk.'

Of an opponent Disraeli said: 'He is like an old goat on Mount Haemus.'

On Lord Brougham: 'The lawyer has spoilt the statesman.'

Of a back-bencher who was not known for his intellect, he remarked: 'He is not so much out of his depth as three miles from the shore.'

His political rival for most of Disraeli's career was William Gladstone about whom he said: 'Posterity will do justice to that unprincipled maniac. An extraordinary mixture of envy, vindictiveness, hypocrisy and superstition; and with one commanding characteristic – whether Prime Minister or Leader of the Opposition, whether preaching, praying, speechifying or scribbling – never a gentleman.'

Later, again on Gladstone: 'It is easy to say he is mad. It looks like it. My theory about him is unchanged: a ceaseless

Tartuffe from the beginning. That sort of man does not go mad at 70.'

But his most famous insulting remark about Gladstone was: 'He is a sophisticated rhetorician, inebriated with the exuberance of his own verbosity and gifted with an egotistical imagination that can at times command an interminable and inconsistent series of arguments to malign an opponent and to glorify himself.'

Commenting on a lawyer MP: 'He was ever illustrating the obvious, explaining the evident, expatiating the common-place.'

On Viscount Palmerston, who became Prime Minister in 1855: 'He is an impostor, utterly exhausted. At best he is only ginger beer and not champagne. He is an old painted pantaloon, very deaf, very blind and with false teeth which would fall out of his mouth when speaking if he did not hesitate and halt so in his talk. Here is a man which the country resolves to associate with energy, wisdom and eloquence – and will until he has tried and failed.' Disraeli's vicious criticism of Palmerston is somewhat at odds with the facts. Palmerston held office for over nine years in all, due mainly to his mastery of Parliament.

He was just as savage in describing Peel, of whom he said: 'A burglar of other intellects. There is no other statesman who has committed political larceny on so grand a scale.' (This gibe led Peel to retort, 'Why, if this is so, has he been ready to unite his political fortunes with mine in office?' – a reference to an incident five years earlier when Disraeli had unwisely written to Peel asking for a ministerial appointment.)

Taking a swipe at those MPs who were rarely at the House: 'Unless you are always there, how can you lead the House of Commons? How can you feel their pulse? How can you know the men?'

On the House of Lords: 'The Lords do not encourage wit and so are obliged to put up with pertness.'

On ruling: 'To govern men you must either excel them in their accomplishments or despise them.'

On himself he said: 'I am the blank page between the Old and the New Testaments.'

Among his many sayings the following are the best:

'The palace is not safe when the cottage is not happy.'

'Youth is a blunder; manhood a struggle; old age a regret.'

'The two greatest stimulants to action are youth and debt.'

'Without party, parliamentary government is impossible.'

'All great political questions end in the tenure of land.'

'Damn your principles – stick to your party.'

'Every man has a right to be conceited until he is successful.'

'No one likes his dependence to be treated with respect, for such treatment forms an unpleasant contrast to his own conduct.'

'It is much easier to be critical than correct.'

'Never trust a gentleman by halves.'

'It destroys one's nerves to be amiable every day to the same human being.'

'Nine-tenths of existing books are nonsense and the clever books are the refutation of that nonsense.'

'An aristocracy is rather apt to exaggerate the qualities and magnify the importance of a plebeian leader.'

'Politics is organized opinion.'

'I make it a rule to believe only what I understand.'

When he told a colleague, 'Be frank and explicit,' he then added 'That is the right line to take when you wish to conceal your own mind and to confuse the minds of others.'

His comment on foreign policy generally, made in 1872, still rings true today: 'The very phrase "foreign affairs" makes an Englishman convinced that the talk is about subjects with which he has no concern.'

On Britain: 'An insular country, subject to fogs and with a powerful middle class.'

On British politics he remarked: 'There is no act of

treachery or meanness of which a political party is not capable – for in politics there is no honour.'

On his opponents: 'As I sat opposite the Treasury bench, the ministers reminded me of one of those marine landscapes not very unusual on the coast of South America. You behold a range of exhausted volcanoes.'

Of political power: 'The major quality of a political leader is the ability to say boo to a goose.'

He once silenced a room by referring to 'the hare-brained chatter of irresponsible frivolity.'

In 1880 Disraeli called a general election, confident of victory. Instead, he lost. Within a few months his health had deteriorated and he died a year later in April 1881. He was 76.

THE LIBERAL Archibald Primrose, fifth Earl of Rosebery, was Queen Victoria's personal choice as Prime Minister when Gladstone resigned for the last time. Early in his career Rosebery declared three ambitions in life: to marry an heiress, to win the Derby and to become Prime Minister. He managed to accomplish all three. The heiress he married was a Rothschild.

He was frequently extremely rude to his in-laws. When he wanted to go to bed, and they did not, he used to snap: 'To your tents, oh, Israel.'

Despite his rudeness to his wife's family, it was widely acknowledged that he was a politician with 'charisma'. However, he ended his own career – and for a decade the prospects of office for his own party – by over-reacting to a lost vote in the House. Instead of tabling a motion of confidence – which he would have won – he went completely over the top, announced the resignation of his entire government and was then badly defeated at the subsequent election.

WHEN TORY Prime Minister Lord Salisbury dismissively referred to the first Asian MP, Mr Naoroji, as 'that black man', his comments caused little comment. Today it would probably be a resigning matter. Salisbury's gibe did, however, lead Gladstone to respond: 'I know Lord Salisbury by sight and I am bound to say that, of the two, Lord Salisbury is the blacker.'

HERBERT HENRY ASQUITH was Liberal Prime Minister for eight years and eight months, the second longest tenure this century. He formed his first government in 1908.

He always used to quote a phrase of Bolingbroke's when asked why he never attacked Bonar Law: 'I never wrestle with a chimney sweep.'

He had no such reservations, however, when it came to Winston Churchill of whom he said: 'He is begotten by froth out of foam.'

His view of the USA: 'It is the land of the long-winded and the short-sighted.'

ANDREW BONAR LAW was elected Conservative Leader in 1911 and Prime Minister in 1922, an office he held for only seven months. Shortly after becoming PM, commenting on the fall of Lloyd George earlier that year, he said: 'My experience is that all Prime Ministers suffer by suppression. Their friends do not tell them the truth; they tell them what they want to hear.'

ALTHOUGH MOST of the vitriol emanates from the Commons their noble Lords are not averse to putting in the verbal knife, although generally their debating style is much more restrained than the lower elected house.

Lord Macaulay, formerly Thomas Babington Macaulay, frequently enlivened a debate in the nineteenth century with his barbs. Commenting about Socrates he said: 'The more I read him, the less I wonder that they poisoned him.'

On the arts: 'No person can be a poet, or even enjoy poetry, without a certain unsoundness of mind.'

On a colleague: 'His imagination resembled the wings of an ostrich. It enabled him to run, though not to soar.'

Among his other quips the following are the best:

'Nothing is so useless as a general maxim.'

'There were gentlemen and there were seamen in the Navy of Charles II. But the seamen were not gentlemen; and the gentlemen were not seamen.'

'I know of no spectacle so ridiculous as the British public in one of its periodical fits of morality.'

LLOYD GEORGE, Britain's Prime Minister during the First World War, held office in one role or another for seventeen years. He was a superb orator. This ability remained with him right to the end of his career, even years after he had lost power.

When he was in his 70s he sat listening to a debate on unemployment regulations in which Sir William Jowitt, the Attorney-General, was replying for the Labour government. Sitting slumped in his place he was apparently taking no notice. Jowitt had been originally elected as a Liberal MP but on being offered a job by Ramsay MacDonald, he abandoned the Liberals to join the Labour Party. Due to the economic situation he was introducing regulations which stated that no unemployed man could draw the dole unless he could prove that he was 'genuinely seeking work'. During his speech, Lloyd George intervened and destroyed the Attorney-General with the barb: 'No one could ever accuse the Right Honourable and learned gentleman of not genuinely seeking work.'

He silenced Sir John Simon, another Liberal defector, with the remark: 'He has twice crossed the floor of the House – each time leaving behind him a trail of slime.'

When told he was a good politician he did not take it as a compliment, but replied: 'A politician is a person whose politics you don't agree with. If you do agree with him, he is a statesman.'

After listening to a fellow politician ranting at a public meeting: 'It is easy to settle the world upon a soap box.'

When asked what made a good speech he shot back: 'The finest eloquence is that which gets things done.'

To someone who said he should proceed cautiously he snapped: 'Don't be afraid to take a big step if one is needed. You can't cross a chasm in two small jumps.'

On Winston Churchill: 'He spoilt himself by reading about Napoleon.'

On Lord Derby: 'He is like a cushion. He always bears the impression of the last man who sat on him.'

On the House of Lords: 'Every man has a House of Lords in his own head. Fears, prejudices, misconceptions – those are the peers.'

And when a Conservative back-bencher claimed that the House of Lords was 'the watchdog of the constitution', Lloyd George amplifying the canine reference shot back: 'You mean it is Mr Balfour's poodle! It fetches and carries for him, it barks for him, it bites anybody that he sets it on to.'

On Bonar Law: 'He was honest to the point of simplicity.'

On Tory Prime Minister Neville Chamberlain: 'Not a bad Lord Mayor of Birmingham in a lean year. A retail mind in a wholesale business.'

On what it's like being Prime Minister: 'There can be no friendship at the top.'

And his one-liners:

'If only a politician had to stand on the planks of his platform – it would be constructed better.'

'In British politics, we call each other honourable men because, in politics, there is no honour.'

🏛

FREDERICK EDWIN SMITH, later Lord Birkenhead, first entered Parliament in 1906. Helped by the fact that on his election the Conservative benches were decimated by the Liberal landslide, he made full use of his powers of oratory in speeches laced with sarcasm and wit to become noticed. His rise through the party ranks was meteoric, but he made what some regard as a bad career move by accepting the post of Lord Chancellor. Although this post carries a seat in the Cabinet and is one of the great offices of state, it necessitates the office bearer sitting in the House of Lords. On becoming Lord Chancellor, therefore, Smith effectively kissed goodbye to any chance he had of becoming Prime Minister.

Lord Beaverbrook summed up the widely held view of Smith's contemporaries when he said: 'His chief enemy has always been his own biting and witty tongue, which spares no man.'

In 1886, whilst a student, 'F E'* sat an exam to be accepted at Harrow but he failed miserably. His mother was later told that his knowledge of classics was not up to the required standard. This uncharacteristic failure rankled with him throughout his career. In 1919 when he was Lord Chancellor, he happened to meet Dr Welldon, the headmaster at Harrow at the time of his failure. Over dinner he attacked the doctor about the incident, declaring that he had been a success in everything he had undertaken in his life except this one exam. Not wishing the argument to develop, Dr Welldon said courteously that the incident was his (the doctor's) failure and added, unwisely, that many mothers came to him to

* Even after he was ennobled as the first Earl of Birkenhead – indeed, right up to his death in 1930 – he was still widely known as 'F E'.

point out how clever their sons really were, but that F E's mother had not done so. F E snapped back: 'There was no need for my mother to tell you the same thing about me as she felt certain you would have discovered it for yourself.' The doctor was deeply embarrassed in front of the assembled guests, as Smith had intended him to be. F E later remarked that 33 years was a long time to wait to get one's own back, but that it had been worth it.

When, during his first campaign in 1906, he was accused of always appearing in court for the licensed trade, 'particularly if the licensees belonged to the Tory Party', he angrily rejected the criticism of his professional integrity. He was particularly irked by the local Liberal leader, Edward Evans, of whom he said: 'Mr Evans, I understand, purveys amongst other things pills. I have not the slightest doubt that he sells pills to Conservatives and Liberals alike. He sells pills and I sell brains and I claim the same right in my profession to choose my customers by the same standards as Mr Evans claims in his.'

At this riposte, Evans said that it was F E's selling of his brains that was just what he complained of, adding that F E 'did not appear to have any left' and 'empty vessels make the most noise'.

Another Liberal candidate, who clashed with F E on the subject of the trade figures, told F E not to be 'pessimistic' about the future. Smith snapped back: 'The only pessimism of which I am conscious at the moment is that which is occasioned by seeing the blind pretentiously putting themselves forward as guides to the blind.' This was a brave response as the Liberal candidate was no other than one A P Thomas, who was a professor of commercial law at Liverpool University!

Referring to Liberal dirty tricks in the 1906 election, he said: 'I do not in the least mind being cheated at cards – but I find it a trifle nauseating if my opponent then proceeds to ascribe his success to the favour of the Most High.'

During his maiden speech he took a vicious swipe at Austin Taylor, a fellow Liverpool MP who, within weeks of being re-elected unopposed as a Conservative had crossed the floor of the House to become a Liberal. F E, alluding to the Liberal's landslide of 1906 said of Taylor: 'He has entered the House, not like his new colleagues, on the crest of a wave, but rather by means of an opportune dive.' In a sarcastic vein, he added: 'Everyone in the House will appreciate his presence because there can be no greater compliment paid to the House by a member than that he should be in their midst when his heart is far away, and it must be clear to all those who know his scrupulous sense of honour that his desire must be at the present moment to be amongst his constituents – who are understood to be at least as anxious to meet him.'

During the same speech, he audaciously took a swipe at Winston Churchill, who had also crossed the floor of the House to join the Liberals before undertaking a number of speaking engagements around Britain. Smith referred to an argument put forward by Winston with the barb: 'The House will recognize the peroration – I rather think it has been at the disposal of both parties in the House before undertaking a provincial tour.'

For a few years after his election he continued to practise at the Bar and there is a wealth of stories of his impudence in court. To one judge who told him that having read F E's pleadings, he was no wiser than when he started, F E snapped back: 'Possibly not my Lord, but you are far better informed.'

To another judge who said that he did not think much of F E's case, F E responded: 'I am sorry to hear that my Lord, but your Lordship will find that the more you hear of it, the more it will grow on you.'

One of the most famous incidents in court occurred when F E demolished a boy's claim for damages after an accident.

He started very sympathetically and asked the young lad to show the court how high he could lift his injured arm. With extreme effort the boy raised it to the level of his shoulder. F E continued: 'Thank you very much. Will you now show us how high you could raise it before the accident?' Innocently, the boy shot his arm high in the air – and lost the case.

On the British constitution Smith remarked: 'Britain is the only country in the world which has at once an uncontrolled constitution and an ineffective second chamber … we have a constitution at the mercy of a momentary gust of parliamentary opinion; and secondly … we have no second chamber equipped with the political and constitutional power to resist such a gust.'

When he was attending a dinner at which he was scheduled to make the final speech he became extremely irritated by the other speakers who were all long-winded and overran their time considerably. When F E's turn came, he rose to his feet and said: 'Ladies and gentlemen, I have prepared two speeches for this evening. One of them is a long speech and the other a short speech. In view of the lateness of the hour, I now intend to deliver them both.'

Having to suffer long-winded after-dinner speeches is an experience all politicians go through. On another occasion, when he was again the last speaker on the card, Smith was once more kept waiting an inordinate length of time. The toastmaster finally called upon F E to give his address, at which point he rose to his feet, said '32 Grosvenor Gardens' and left.

Once he was invited to breakfast by the young undergraduate Bob Boothby. He arrived and sat in silence for several minutes before finally remarking: 'Except for one melancholy occasion at 10 Downing Street, this is the first time I have breakfasted in company for 20 years – and I hope to God it is the last.'

In 1919 King George V was informed of an intended

reshuffle in the coalition government led by Lloyd George and there was one appointment which he tried, at first, to block. The PM announced that he wished to promote Sir Frederick Smith, the Attorney-General, to the position of Lord Chancellor. The King's secretary, Lord Stamfordham, protested, firstly on the grounds of Smith's age (46) adding, 'His Majesty feels the appointment will come as somewhat of a surprise to the legal profession ... His Majesty does not feel that Sir Frederick has established such a reputation in men's minds as to ensure the country will welcome him to the second highest post which can be occupied by a subject of the crown.'

Lloyd George, however, held out, the King eventually gave way and Smith took his seat on the Woolsack as the first Lord Birkenhead. To the surprise of many, including the King, Smith gave the post a dignified presence. He disliked tempering justice with levity and, when sitting as a Lord of Appeal, he prided himself that no observation he ever made was followed by laughter in court.

However, once out of legal robes, he was just as insulting, rude and flippant as he had ever been. Shortly after his elevation as Lord Chancellor, he was invited on board the Royal Yacht *Britannia* at Cowes. Having dined rather well he started to puff smoke from a huge cigar into the Queen's face until a courtier eventually persuaded him to go on deck to see the stars.

When it was suggested by the King's secretary, Stamfordham, that he ought to ask the King's permission before going abroad, he wrote what the King considered 'a very rude letter'. He angrily cited constitutional precedent for coming and going as he pleased and concluded his remarks by saying, 'You will assure the King, with my deep respect, that if he would wish to be consulted as to my brief absences, after seven months' arduous and unbroken labour, I should, of course, consider it my duty to take his Majesty's pleasure.'

Later, when being entertained by Lord Beaverbrook, someone inquired as to the vintage of the claret they were drinking and wanted to know what vineyard it was from. 'I can tell straight away by its distinctive taste,' Smith intervened, 'it's from the local grocer's.'

Jimmy Thomas, the railwaymen's leader who had been elected as an MP in 1910, was often the butt of F E's insults. Rather surprisingly the two became friends, although this did not prevent Smith from continuing to needle Thomas who was notorious for not pronouncing his aitches. Once, when Thomas complained of 'an 'orrible 'eadache,' Smith replied: 'What you need, my dear chap, is a couple of aspirates.'

Whilst attending a luncheon in Swansea to mark the opening of the new Town Hall, he found himself sitting next to the Prince of Wales. They both had to sit through a very long-winded speech by the Mayor and the Prince uttered to Smith: 'I wish there was some way of stopping this dreadful bore.' At this, F E picked up the menu card, wrote a few words on the back and asked the toastmaster to give it to the speaker. Shortly after he had done this, the Mayor made some very brief closing remarks and sat down. The Prince was amazed that F E's note had done the trick and asked him what he had written. 'Oh nothing much,' Smith replied, 'I just told him his fly buttons were undone.'

Among his best-remembered barbs are the following:

On Austen Chamberlain: 'He always played the game – and he always lost.'

Commenting on the Cabinet of Conservative Prime Minister Andrew Bonar Law (of which he was not a member): 'He tried to confront first-class problems with a team of second-class brains.'

On politics: 'To say what is not is the road to success.'

His view of the Liberal Party: 'Political Rip Van Winkles.'

And of a speech by Hilaire Belloc: 'The more often I hear it, the more I like it.'

BENJAMIN DISRAELI: 'My idea of an agreeable person is a person who agrees with me.'

Commenting on an ugly opponent: 'The arguments he produces in his election address will win no more votes than his photograph on the front cover.'

His gibe to the Liverpool Liberal leader Edward Evans: 'He is the greatest asset his opponents enjoy and I for one wish him many more years of pretentious pompousness and fussy failure.'

'Votes are to swords exactly what bank notes are to gold. The one is effective only because the other is believed to lie behind it.'

On Churchill (before he and F E became friends): 'He has been hungering and thirsting for office and will take anything he is offered. As for Lord Beaverbrook, he would have given his eyes for the Board of Trade.'

On Stanley Baldwin's first Cabinet: 'It is, of course, a tragedy that so great an army should have so uninspiring a commander-in-chief.'

On the 1925 coal dispute: 'I should have thought that the miners' leaders were the stupidest men in the kingdom – if I had not met the owners.'

Referring to the lavish entertaining undertaken by the Marquis of Londonderry before his promotion to high government office, F E caustically observed that Londonderry had 'catered his way to the Cabinet'.

Commenting on the breaking off of diplomatic relations with the USSR in 1927: 'I am delighted. We have got rid of the hypocrisy of pretending to have friendly relations with this gang of murderers, revolutionaries and thieves. I breathe quite differently now we have purged our capital of the unclean and treacherous elements.'

And in response to those who were arguing for a cut in Britain's armed forces he said: 'Is the ownership of the world to be stereotyped by perpetual tenure in the hands of those who possess the different territories today? The world continues to offer glittering prizes to those who have stout arms and sharp swords, and it is therefore extremely improbable that the experience of future nations will differ in any material respect from that which has happened since the dawn of the human race.'

Right to the end of his life F E had quite a good head of hair. On one occasion some five years before he died he went for a haircut and the barber, who was totally bald, made the unwise observation: 'Getting a little thin at the back, sir.' He was withered by F E's retort: 'I do not think that a man of your limited resources is really in a position to comment.' Then, when asked how he would like his hair to be cut, he snapped: 'In silence.'

In 1928 returning to England after a trip abroad he found himself on the same boat as Randolph Churchill, Winston's son. The journey on the *Berengaria* took several days and F E was asked to deliver a speech at the ship's concert to make an appeal for funds for distressed mariners.

He willingly obliged but was extremely disappointed by the collection. The following evening when he was playing bridge with Churchill, the chief steward, carrying a large wastepaper basket full of dollar bills, approached two American women at a nearby table. F E overheard the steward say to the ladies, 'Here are your winnings from the pool on the ship's run.' He noticed there appeared to be about fifteen hundred dollars in the wastepaper basket.

Still irritated by the relative failure of his appeal the night before, he turned to the ladies and said: 'How much did you give to the appeal which I delivered last night?' One of them replied: 'We gave twenty dollars each.' Smith rose to his feet and snapped: 'Inadequate.' He then put his hand into the wastepaper basket and handed to the chief steward the large wad he had indiscriminately grabbed, saying: 'Tell the purser to add this extra contribution to my appeal from the two ladies who won the pool tonight.'

According to Churchill, the two women looked furious

but were so shocked that they did not remonstrate with Smith or complain to the ship's captain.

During the summer of 1930 Smith fell seriously ill with bronchial pneumonia and died on 30 September that year.

Despite the insults F E heaped on Stanley Baldwin, his old boss had long since forgotten their differences, saying when news of his death was announced: 'For four years his counsel in cabinet was invaluable. In dark days he was a tower of strength.' Despite his spectacular faults and barbed tongue, which spared no one, most were willing to forgive, preferring to recall his wise judgement rather than his rude insolence.

Although he achieved much, looking back over Smith's career one cannot help feeling a sense of waste. His epitaph is perhaps best summed up by the words of Geoffrey Chaucer, who over five hundred years earlier remarked: 'When a man has an over-great wit, often he will misuse it.'

F E'S LONG-TIME friend, Sir Edward Carson showed he had a self-deprecating style. On being made minister responsible for naval affairs in 1916 he said: 'My only great qualification for being put in charge of the Navy is that I am very much at sea.'

STANLEY BALDWIN never expected to become Prime Minister, but from the time he achieved that high office in 1923 until he quit active politics altogether in 1937, he proved to be a dominating influence in Britain causing Winston Churchill to describe him as 'the most formidable politician I have ever known'.

His down-to-earth approach was at the time most unusual for a Tory politician. Although his laid-back style was not to everyone's taste many found it a refreshing change. His manner made him popular with the public and for a time he had an unassailable hold on the House of Commons.

Baldwin was not too reticent to express his views on his contemporaries. In 1933 Winston Churchill, then a back-bencher, was seeking to reverse the British government's policy on India and this set him on a collision course with Baldwin. Their previous relationship, although not cordial, was amiable enough. Now, as a result of Churchill's campaigning, the two men no longer spoke to one another. One day, after leaving the chamber, Churchill entered a small lavatory reserved for MPs which only had enough room for two men to relieve themselves at the same time. He saw to his embarrassment that one of the 'pissoirs' was occupied by Baldwin. As Baldwin had noticed him entering, he felt it was too late to retreat. Baldwin remained silent but as he did up his trousers, he turned to Churchill and snapped: 'I am glad that there is one common platform upon which we can still meet,' and walked off.

He continued to have a low regard for Britain's future war leader describing him as: 'A military adventurer who would sell his sword to anyone. He has his sentimental side, but he lacks soul.'

And his last words on Churchill: 'When Winston was born, lots of fairies swooped down on his cradle and gave him gifts – imagination, eloquence, industry and ability. Then came the fairy who said "No one person has a right to so many gifts," picked him up and gave him a shake and a twist and despite all these gifts, he was denied judgement and wisdom. And that is why, while we delight to listen to him in the House, we do not take his advice.'

Baldwin never liked or trusted Lloyd George either. When the latter was Chancellor of the Exchequer he said of him: 'He is a mere shadow of his former self, wandering in a sort of Celtic twilight, his only intention being to rob hen roosts.'

During this time, when he served as Chancellor of the Exchequer and before the First World War, Lloyd George acquired the nickname of 'the goat'. This led Baldwin to quote an old Afghan proverb regularly behind Lloyd George's back: 'He who lies in the bosom of the goat spends his remaining years plucking out the fleas.'

Showing contempt for the description of a colleague as 'brilliant' he said: 'Brilliance appears to be synonymous with a rapid capacity for changing one's ground to suit one's convenience.'

On his role as Leader of the Opposition: 'Leading the Conservative Party is like driving pigs to market.'

On Lord Birkenhead (F E Smith): 'He attached himself very cleverly to the strings of Austen Chamberlain's apron. Austen is one of those loyal men who could not see disloyalty or intrigue even if it was at his elbow.'

When F E Smith described Lloyd George as 'a dynamic force' Stanley Baldwin riposted: 'Yes, and it is from that very fact that our troubles arise. A dynamic force is a very terrible thing; it may crush you and it is not necessarily right.'

On the press barons Lord Beaverbrook and Lord Rothermere: 'They are men I would not have in my house. I do not respect them. Who are they?'

Baldwin on Socialism: 'No gospel founded on hate will ever be the gospel of our people.'

His comments on a back-bencher: 'He nailed his colours firmly to the fence – and abstained.'

Following the Liberals' decision to leave the national government in 1931, he echoed the thoughts of many Conservatives about the Liberal Party when he said: 'The dirty dogs. They always behave like this when rough weather approaches.'

Of Ramsay MacDonald, towards the end of the latter's tenure as Prime Minister of the national government: 'It was tragic to see him in his closing days as PM, losing the thread of his speech and turning to ask colleagues why people were laughing – he became detested by his old friends and despised by the Conservatives.' Indeed, MacDonald became such a pathetic figure that his long-time friend Lady Londonderry came to refer to him as 'Ramshackle Mac'.

On fellow Cabinet minister Leo Amery: 'He does not add a gram to the influence of the government.'

This led Amery to say of Baldwin: 'He was emotional, impulsive, secretive and intensely personal in his likes and dislikes. He was profoundly illogical and intuitive, browsing over a problem until the vague cloud of his thoughts condensed into some conclusion. By nature indolent, his inertia was fortified by a profound scepticism as to the results of any particular administrative action.'

After the General Strike of 1926, Baldwin indeed appeared to be overtaken by a sort of mental inertia. This led to one colleague saying of him: 'Sick in body, far more sick in mind', whilst Neville Chamberlain referred to occasions when Baldwin 'went completely out of gear and started sniffing blotting paper'. Even the then relatively junior MP Harold Macmillan referred to the PM as 'losing his grip on the situation'.

Lord Derby said of him: 'He can make extraordinarily good speeches and everyone likes him, but he has got absolutely no drive. The worst of him is his leadership. He has no hold on his party. He listens to all the agreeable things that are said and not to any of the disagreeable ones. He is living in a fools' paradise.'

Derby's view was shared by Austen Chamberlain who commented: 'Baldwin's leadership was always "the accident of an accident". Never has any party been more patient with incapacity; never has any man been given so many chances and pulled out of the water so many times; but I think that at last the end has come and that the party will be forced to get rid of its old man of the sea if it is not prepared to be drowned by him.'

Chamberlain later said of him: 'A man so unstable of

purpose and so muddled of mind. He does not fit in at any point with the picture which the public have made of him for themselves. They think him a simple, hardworking, unambitious man, not a "politician" in the abusive sense in which they so often use the word, whom nothing but a stern sense of duty keeps at his ungrateful task, a man too of wide and liberal mind who has educated his party. I know him as self-centred, selfish and idle, yet one of the shrewdest politicians, but without a constructive idea in his head and with an amazing ignorance of Indian and foreign affairs and of the real values of political life. "Sly – devilishly sly!" would be my chapter heading and egotism and idleness the principal characteristic that I should assign to him.'

A parliamentary colleague once said of Baldwin that 'He always hit the nail on the head – but it never seemed to go any further.' However, even towards the end of his career, Winston Churchill did not agree with all the criticism, saying: 'They talk of the honest stupid Baldwin, but believe me he is the most ruthless and astute politician of our day.'

Towards the end of his last administration he did draw some criticism from Churchill, who accused his government of drift for failing to keep his pledge to improve Britain's air power. Churchill said: 'The government simply cannot make up their minds, or they cannot persuade the Prime Minister to make up his mind ... So we go on preparing for months and years – precious, perhaps vital, to the greatness of Britain – for the locusts to eat.'

When, on retiring as Prime Minister he was asked by Sir Henry 'Chips' Channon what it had been like, he replied: 'When I get out of here, I'll sleep for a week,' adding: 'here I've been for fifteen years going down to the House to answer fatuous questions.'

On leaving office, he was asked by a journalist whether he would be available to give his successor the benefit of his opinions. His retort was not only worthy of note, but even today is excellent advice for ex-Prime Ministers! 'Once I leave, I leave. I am not going to speak to the man on the bridge, and I am not going to spit on the deck.'

Baldwin singularly failed to impress his predecessor Bonar Law, who summed up his successor in one sentence: 'His defect was too much modesty.'

LORD CURZON was a talented but arrogant politician who, even in his day, was regarded as somewhat out of touch. In an age when politicians were usually treated with deference by the press, he very nearly became Prime Minister. In the event, he lost out to Stanley Baldwin and never recovered from the fact, many of his comments containing more than a hint of sour grapes.

Despite his bitter disappointment he served as Baldwin's Foreign Secretary, but showed little gratitude to his boss of whom he remarked: 'It is heart-breaking serving under such a man. He is guilty of ... a mixture of innocence, ignorance, honesty and stupidity – fatal gifts in a statesman when wholly disassociated from imagination, vision or *savoir faire*. He is a man of the utmost insignificance.'

On the Cabinet of which he was a member: 'They secretly grumble. Baldwin's evil geniuses are the whippersnappers of the Cabinet, Amery and Neville Chamberlain. They buzz about him day and night and he is lamentably weak.'

And his terse view of F E Smith: 'What a cad the man is!'

LORD DERBY commenting in 1923: 'Europe is dominated by the mad men – Poincaré* and Mussolini – and England is ruled by a damned idiot.' (He meant Stanley Baldwin.)

* The French leader.

WINSTON CHURCHILL who never looked at television on a regular basis had little regard for the medium saying: 'Why do we need this peepshow?' He went on to add that the BBC was 'Honeycombed with Socialists – probably with Communists. It is nothing more than a nest of Communist sympathizers, an enemy within the gates, doing more harm than good.'

And on the possibility of television covering politics (in the early years of TV there was no coverage of elections or of any controversial news subject): 'It would be a shocking thing to have the debates of Parliament forestalled on this new robot organization.'

His view of the prospect of commercial television was contemptuous: 'It would be nothing more than a twopenny Punch and Judy show.'

And when the Director-General of the BBC John (later Lord) Reith insisted that BBC broadcasts during the General Strike in 1926 had to be 'impartial' Churchill exploded. 'This argument is ill-considered. You have no right to be impartial between the fire and the fire brigade.'

FORMER LABOUR PREMIER Clement Attlee had advice for those who, like today's Euro-rebels, were clamouring for a referendum. He described it as 'a device of dictators and demagogues'.

He had a dim view of television, saying: 'It is nothing more than an idiot's lantern.'

WHEN ASKED to deliver a speech by reading from a tele-prompter, former Conservative Prime Minister Harold Mac-millan declined, adding: 'As I am very short-sighted, I could just manage to read the words if I screwed up my eyes. I would present the appearance of a corpse looking out of the window.'

Alluding to the number of Jews Margaret Thatcher appointed to her Cabinet he commented: 'The Cabinet has more Estonians than Etonians.'

On Neville Chamberlain, one of his predecessors: 'In his earlier days, his undoubted intellectual arrogance was partly concealed. After he became Prime Minister, and especially after Munich, it developed almost to a form of mania. Yet at all times he was a difficult man to argue with. In debate he was seldom conciliatory and generally unyielding. He knew he was right on every question. Baldwin was never quite sure that anybody was right, especially himself. Baldwin's approach to problems was largely one of temperament and feeling. Chamberlain brought to them a clear, logical and sometimes ruthless mind. Nor did he take any trouble to make himself agreeable even to his supporters, still less to his opponents. He seldom, if ever, joined in the camaraderie of the House of Commons. He was, in Dr Johnson's phrase, an "unclubbable man".'

When Macmillan sacked a number of his ministers in a reshuffle, one of those dismissed, Lord Kilmuir, complained that 'A cook would have been given more notice of his dismissal.' This led to the riposte from Macmillan: 'Ah, but good cooks are hard to find.'

Macmillan summed up much of parliamentary debate when he said: 'I have never found, in a long experience of politics, that criticism is ever inhibited by ignorance.'

Before being insulting it is worth giving some thought to the words to be used. Insults can and do back-fire. It happened during the late fifties to two critics of Harold Macmillan. The Socialist cartoonist Vicky sarcastically called him 'Supermac' in an attempt to deflate his soaring popularity. Later, Labour politician Nye Bevan referred to one of Macmillan's policy initiatives as 'Macwonder'. In both cases the gibes rebounded and, like the 'iron lady', Mrs Thatcher, some twenty years later, Macmillan became a beneficiary from, and not a casualty of, the attempted vituperation.

RICHARD AUSTEN BUTLER is only the second politician this century to be known widely and universally by his initials.* 'Rab' twice almost became Prime Minister, but was regarded as 'unsound' by many Conservative right-wingers, some of whom referred to him as 'a milk and water Socialist'. Indeed, others claimed that Rab was so left-wing that his views were identical to those of the then Labour leader Hugh Gaitskell. This led to his vision of Conservatism being snidely described as 'Butskellism', an insult which provided grist to the mill of the opponents of both men.

His critics also claimed that he behaved more like a civil servant than a politician. However, this insult contained a hint of a back-handed compliment, recognizing his undoubted gift for management.

Usually his speeches were constructive and well argued. He generally preferred to make out a good case for what he was doing rather than rely on the political barb or low insult. It was precisely this quality which led even his supporters to despair of him. They said with some justification that his speeches lacked 'punch' and that he 'lacked the killer instinct'. Certainly many political observers feel, if he had made the effort, he could have succeeded Macmillan to the Conservative Party leadership in 1963.

Despite his generally polite manner he did on occasions resort to the insulting gibe or discomforting comment, although even at his worst he was still positively diplomatic by comparison with Norman Tebbit.

* The other was Frederick Edwin Smith, later the first Earl of Birkenhead who was universally known as 'F E' (see page 18).

His solemn demeanour in public was often misleading. He did have a highly developed sense of humour and would sometimes deliberately make ambiguous remarks when even his friends could not be sure whether he was being serious or not. His comment at Heathrow Airport on Eden is an example in point. (See page 38.)

When a right-wing Conservative appeared oblivious to the effects of deflation, he retorted: 'Those like you who talk about creating pools of unemployment should be thrown into them and made to swim.'

Dismissing a group of Tory rebels who were opposed to Stanley Baldwin he dubbed them 'the forty thieves', whilst of fellow Tory Winston Churchill he remarked: 'He is a half-breed American and the greatest political adventurer of modern times.'

He did not like Lord Beaverbrook, saying: 'I found him green and apeish.'

On Harold Macmillan: 'He is the Restoration Monarch of modern times. He has an infinite capacity for elasticity which might tire his friends, if they did not realize that he is ruthless in his determination to carry the disaffected along with him at all costs.'

On the Labour Party's 1945 electoral triumph: 'Their success was like a bout of measles which the country would have to suffer but from which there was no doubt that the British people would ultimately pull through.'

His view of Harold Wilson: 'He was adept at using the smear as a political weapon.'

He referred to the House of Commons as: 'A form of riding school, in which individual horses prance around but in which the ultimate decision and march of events is left to the riding master, in the shape of the government.'

On Sir Samuel Hoare MP, former Secretary of State for India: 'I was amazed by his ambitions; I admired his imagination, I stood in awe of his intellectual capacity, but I was never touched by his humanity. He was the coldest fish with whom I ever had to deal.'

On the Marquess of Zetland, Secretary of State for India in 1935: 'He was too punctilious to be informal and too straightlaced to be communicative.' This was a view he reached whilst serving under Zetland as a junior minister in the India Office. Indeed, to call Zetland straightlaced was something of an understatement. Rab was required to seek an appointment in writing if he wished to see his own boss!

Of Edward VIII he said: 'He was a congenitally weak man but with great personal charm.'

On David Fleming MP, Solicitor-General for Scotland between the First and Second World Wars, he said: 'He may have been a distinguished Scottish judge but I had not been prepared for the limitations of his views or for the humourlessness with which he gave them rein.'

On former Prime Minister Sir Alec Douglas-Home, who became Leader of the Conservative Party in 1963, when many thought that Rab would be chosen: 'An amiable enough creature – however, I am afraid he doesn't understand economics or even education at all.'

And taking a further swipe at Sir Alec, with more than a hint of bitterness, he remarked: 'I may never have known much about ferrets or flower arranging, but one thing I did know is how to govern the people of this country.'

During his period as Master of Trinity College he said to a retiring Clerk of Works: 'My wife and I are to glad to have got here in time to see you leave.' Those around him could not be sure whether he meant to be insulting or whether it was a mistake, but the clerk in question was offended.

On another occasion he was invited to the retirement dinner of Lord Fraser of Kilmorach. He replied declining, but adding 'There is no one I would rather attend a farewell meeting for than Lord Fraser.'

During the early part of Sir Anthony Eden's premiership – before the fiasco of Suez – some newspapers began to speculate on Eden's future. Caught by a journalist at Heathrow Airport who asked him to comment on the press reports, Rab uttered what was to become his most famous remark ever. When asked whether he supported Eden, he replied: 'He is the best Prime Minister we have.'

Some political commentators thought such remarks were uttered quite innocently, but those who knew him well think differently. Indeed, his friends believe that this waspish irreverence prevented him from becoming leader of the Conservative Party, a view supported by Professor Galbraith who feels that it was Rab's habit of looking on others with 'ill-concealed amusement' that stopped him reaching the very top.

Although many of his colleagues felt that he was unfairly denied the premiership, not everyone was a fan of Rab. During the war, the Conservative MP for Chichester, Major J S Courtauld, said of him: 'He's industrious but loopy.'

HAROLD (NOW LORD) WILSON is the most successful leader the Labour Party has had. He led his party to victory in the general elections of 1964, 1966 and 1974, failing only once, in 1970, when he lost to Ted Heath.

A significant element of Wilson's success was undoubtedly his ability to manage the Labour Party effectively and prevent damaging splits between the left and right wings. Wilson had the knack of papering over the cracks, and has candidly admitted how he did it: 'Leading the Labour Party is like driving an old stage coach. If it is rattling along at a rare old speed, most of the passengers are so exhilarated – perhaps even seasick – they don't start arguing or quarrelling. As soon as it stops, they start arguing about which way to go. The trick is to keep it going at an exhilarating speed.'

His preoccupation with keeping Labour together soon led his detractors to accuse him of pursuing expediency rather than formulated policy. Indeed, some would say that the views he has expressed on Benjamin Disraeli could equally apply to his own career. Of Disraeli he commented: 'He had a complete and almost proverbial lack of political principle, often acting by instinct.'

Of one of his predecessors, former Labour leader George Lansbury, Wilson has said: 'He was a much loved, dedicated pacifist, but totally unsuited to the responsibilities of leadership.'

He has also made less than complimentary comments on the following:

Of Stanley Baldwin: 'He was the antithesis of Lloyd George. He would conduct the orchestra and not tire himself. He was the finely tuned manipulator of the steering wheel: direction without engine power, the prerogative of the bosun through out the ages.'

On Neville Chamberlain: 'It was not only that he was totally inadequate as Prime Minister: many are and some get by. What was tragic was that he was totally opinionated, totally certain he was right.'

On Ramsay MacDonald, Labour's first Prime Minister: 'He still embodies a legend of betrayal to the Labour Party, without having secured a word of tribute. He gradually became a pathetic figure, tired, ill, rambling and taking refuge in virtually meaningless and almost unending phrases.'

And Wilson on the Liberal Party at the end of the last century: 'Gladstone clung to the leadership and an increasingly rebellious party simply did not dare to get rid of him. No one would bell the cat.'

He did not think much of Britain's nineteenth-century Prime Minister Lord Aberdeen, of whom he said: 'As a leader he was weak and unfit for the premiership.'

On Herbert Morrison, who served in Clem Attlee's Labour

government: 'He was not so much disloyal as watching for a favourable opportunity to be disloyal.'

On former Conservative Prime Minister Anthony Eden: 'He was one of the great gentlemen of British politics – and one of the great tragedies. He had a jealous temperament.'

And on former Tory Prime Minister Harold Macmillan: 'Macmillan's role as a poseur was itself a pose. He was a patrician in a non-patrician age, a dedicated professional who gave the impression of effortless government. He was one of the most articulate of Britain's premiers who regarded the premiership as a source of continuous enjoyment. He was a Disraelian, perhaps the last Disraelian Prime Minister Britain will see.'

In 1960, when he was Labour's Shadow Chancellor, Wilson criticized Macmillan's running of the economy saying of him: 'He is the creator of the candy floss society. Had the trade cycle never existed, he would have invented it and used it for his electoral purposes. As Chancellor and Prime Minister he played the cycle.'

But his most effective put-down of Macmillan was the barb: 'He had an expensive education. Eton and Suez.'

Of politics generally he said: 'One of the laws of politics is that nothing provocative must be allowed to occur in an allied country in the year leading up to an American presidential election.' (Wilson undoubtedly had the Suez crisis in mind as the main example of this maxim.)

On former Labour Chancellor Hugh Dalton: 'Apart from his loud voice, he had little to commend him. He had an infinite capacity for meeting himself coming back.'

Commenting on veteran Labour minister, James Griffiths, former Secretary of State for Wales: 'He was a cross between a charter-mayor and an arch-Druid figure.'

On political power: 'Every statesman should remember his power to evoke a reaction-coefficient greater than unity.'

His view of the qualities required of a Prime Minister: 'No

EDWARD HEATH ON ENOCH POWELL: 'He was some-
times brilliant, but mostly all you hear is the buzzing of the
bees in his bonnet.'

one should attempt the role of PM who cannot fall asleep the moment he is in bed with the cares and worries of the day behind him.'

Defending his own approach to the job of PM: 'A healer does not usually get a good press. Fleet Street thrives on confrontation. If a Prime Minister uses his political skills to keep the Cabinet together in pursuit of a common aim and common policies, he is condemned as devious; if he forces splits and public recriminations then, as long as he takes the right side in the division, he is a hero – but his Cabinet disintegrates.'

And expanding on his theme of the PM's office: 'True Prime Ministership lies somewhere between Sir Robert Peel and Lord John Russell: you cannot ignore your party, or the particular views of individual ministers – but equally you cannot put the Prime Minister's position into commission. The trouble with Russell is there was no central direction. Even his most cherished measures were subject to amendment by any parliamentary faction. This was open government, but the emphasis was more on "open" than on government. He was more like a Speaker than a Prime Minister.'

Attacking former Tory Prime Minister Sir Alec Douglas-Home, he remarked: 'He is the grouse moor conception of Tory leadership. We should have a society in which brains take precedence over blue blood.' This led Sir Alec to respond referring to Labour's inverted snobbery with: 'Labour are as stuffy and dated as a Victorian front room.'

On P G Wodehouse: 'He had a naive insistence on visiting Hitler's Berlin and broadcasting unpatriotic claptrap on their radio during the war.'

Throughout most of Wilson's time at Number 10, he faced Ted Heath as Leader of the Opposition, about whom he said: 'A shiver looking for a spine to run up.'

Early in 1972 there was a political row when unemployment passed the one million mark. Wilson by this time was in

Opposition and the Prime Minister was Edward Heath. Heath had just returned from the EEC negotiations in Brussels which led Wilson to gibe: 'He is the first dole queue millionaire to cross the channel since Neville Chamberlain.'

On the 1972 miners' strike: 'This is Mr Heath's crisis. His government was determined to have a showdown. They have set their stern hard-hearted faces against any prices and incomes policy and have gone in for this virility contest.'

Back in power after the 1974 general election* Wilson faced a difficult public expenditure round with a slender parliamentary majority. When the vote came, a number of left-wing MPs abstained, which caused the Labour government to lose the motion on public expenditure. Some defended their actions by saying that they could have voted with the Conservatives, but didn't. Wilson, who was furious, snapped: 'It is always an arguable question about promiscuity whether one is more open to criticism for going into the bedroom or being the lap dog outside the door.'

He went on to refer to the comfort that the Labour left-wingers had given to the Conservatives as 'An unholy parliamentary alliance that can only be described as arsenic and red chiffon.'†

On his then Industry Minister Tony Benn: 'Tony has some of the qualities of an Old Testament prophet without the beard. He rambles on about the new Jerusalem.'

He dismissed his Cabinet colleagues with the comment: 'Few politicians are masochists.'

Despite Wilson's considerable success over the years at the ballot box, his former Cabinet colleague Richard Crossman was not impressed: 'Harold Wilson had one overriding aim —

---

* There were two general elections in 1974 and although the results of both were close, Labour managed to form an administration after four years of Conservative rule.

† This recalls F E Smith's comment on the Shinwell–Winterton alliance as 'arsenic and old lace'.

to remain in office. He would use almost every trick or gimmick to achieve it. Whenever I go to see Harold, I look into those grey eyes – and see nothing.'

BEFORE HE entered full-time politics, Tory Prime Minister Edward Heath was offered a job by Lord Reith of the BBC. He turned it down with the barb: 'I couldn't work for God Almighty.'

On former BBC Director-General Sir Hugh Greene he was even more insulting: 'A frightful man. It was his fashion to knock things down and doubt a man's integrity.'

During a tour of north-east England in February 1969, whilst driving through the slums of Newcastle, Heath surprised an aide when he remarked: 'If I lived here, I wouldn't vote for Harold Wilson.' He paused and then added: 'And I wouldn't vote for myself either – I'd vote for Robespierre.'

Many feel that he has never fully come to terms with his defeat as leader of the Conservative Party by Margaret Thatcher in 1975. Shortly afterwards, he said of the party he once led: 'What we've got in the party now is PR men, men in advertising. All sorts of people have got selected by local committees who probably never expected to get into Parliament at all. I don't believe what we've got now is true Conservatism. It's 1860s' *laissez-faire* Liberalism that never was. All that telling people to get on their bikes and find a job – what's the use of telling the ex-steel workers of Consett to get on their bikes? Where on earth would they go?'

And Heath in a similar vein: 'The answer to unemployment is better organization. I think Churchill would have been appalled at Mrs Thatcher's government.'

On the Labour Party he is rather more terse: 'It is a shambles.'

When a supporter criticized him for the fact that he was unmarried, he snapped back: 'What I do know is that a man who got married in order to be a better Prime Minister wouldn't be either a good Prime Minister or a good husband.'

🏛

HAROLD WILSON'S successor as Prime Minister was James Callaghan. Almost immediately he entered Number 10 in 1976 he faced a sterling crisis. Of the currency speculators at the time he said: 'They behaved with all the restraint of schoolgirls at a rock concert.'

His hopes of winning the 1979 general election were dashed by the 1978 winter of discontent about which he commented: 'One of the most notorious excesses was the refusal of Liverpool grave-diggers to bury the dead, accounts of which appalled the country when they saw pictures of mourners being turned away from the cemetery. Such heart-lessness and cold-blooded indifference to the feelings of families at moments of intense grief, rightly aroused deep revulsion and did untold harm to the cause of trade unionism, which I, like many others, had been proud to defend through-out my life.'

🏛

SIR GERALD NABARRO, the late flamboyant Tory back-bencher may have been a pain in the neck to his party's Whips during his period in the House, but he certainly enlivened many a debate with his vivid turn of insult.

He won wide support for his comments on tabloid journal-ists: 'Their articles are garbled, inaccurate, lurid in character and collected by men who are only interested in sensational journalism of doubtful validity.'

On his colleagues when they appeared on television: 'Most MPs could no more remember what they said in a television interview a week ago than fly to the moon.'

On outmoded attitudes by British management: 'In the post-war world in Britain it has been considered in many circles to be slightly "off" to be eager, slightly improper to be thrusting, not done to be ambitious. Quite simply, these sentiments are drivel.'

And on his party leader Edward Heath: 'The cartoonists find him easy to draw because he has facial idiosyncrasies. He has a pudgy face and sticking out of it a very sharp nose and these two features are sharply opposed.'

Seeing a middle-aged member of the public using a telephone reserved for MPs, Nabarro grabbed the man by the scruff of the neck, bellowed, 'These phones are for use by MPs only,' and called over a security guard to remove the offending miscreant. It was then pointed out to him that the person he had just assaulted was Hugh McCartney, a Labour Member of Parliament. Unabashed, Nabarro walked off muttering: 'Well he's never bloody here anyway.'

He was a good platform orator but towards the end his ego became something of a problem. Lord Waddington remembers with horror one occasion when he heard Nabarro speak. 'He was doing quite well until about halfway through the speech he suddenly left the stage and started walking round the hall. Every so often he would stop when he reached a table where an attractive woman was sitting and he would put his hand on her shoulder, pause for a few minutes and then wander off to the next table. It was both appalling and embarrassing,' he recalls.

He had become an unashamed self-publicist who was more interested in getting himself on television than in dealing with the issues of the day. However, on one particular occasion he managed to use the media to great effect to ensure that the then Labour government did not increase taxes on the British motorist.

Suspecting that in view of Britain's dire economic position the Chancellor of the Exchequer Roy Jenkins would be obliged to increase taxes – including an increase in vehicle excise duty – Nabarro, who was Chairman of the House of

Commons Motor Club, made a spectacular claim that he was the recipient of a Budget leak that there was going to be an increase in the vehicle excise duty from the then annual amount of £25 to at least £35 – a colossal increase at the time. Nabarro's publicity was so effective that Prime Minister Harold Wilson took the unprecedented step of setting up a Select Committee to examine the allegations of a breach of Budget secrecy.

One MP, Labour's former thespian Andrew Faulds, was against the setting up of the Select Committee arguing that it was 'a waste of time to inquire into the tittle-tattle of such a self-publicist as that cardboard cavalier'. This led Nabarro to raise a point of order with the Speaker, during which he referred to Faulds as 'a broken-down actor from Stratford on Avon'.

Despite Fauld's objections the inquiry went ahead. Initially, Nabarro had told the press that Treasury officials had leaked the Chancellor's intentions, but when faced with interrogation by the Select Committee, he back-pedalled saying that all he had intended to convey was his opinion that, having read Treasury economic forecasts, he concluded that excise duty 'would be increased'. He went on to say that 'two visitors' to the central lobby had then shown to him a document which was a draft application form for taxing a motor vehicle, which contained the new tax tables. Whilst the investigation proceeded, Nabarro issued press release after press release, insisting that the Labour government was going to hit the British motorist severely.

As the investigation proceeded, his rhetoric became more detached from the evidence and the Select Committee – which included Conservative members – concluded that there was no Budget leak and that his allegations were groundless. This was a severe rebuke to Nabarro, the implication being that he had been, at best, naive and gullible, at worst, less than honest in the comments he had made.

Not many parliamentary careers could have survived such a rebuke. Showing a colossal amount of chutzpah and an equal measure of cheek, he immediately went on television to proclaim the result as a victory. At least one television interviewer was nonplussed by Nabarro's braggadocio and asked him how he could say this when the Select Committee had refuted his allegations. Without blinking an eyelid Nabarro roared: 'A defeat? Just let's see them put up the car tax now!'

His campaign worked: car tax was not increased that year. But there was a heavy price to pay. He was never again taken seriously by his colleagues.

I must admit that I have a sneaking regard for someone with this level of brazen cheek. However, at least two of my colleagues who were contemporaries of Nabarro have a different view. 'The man was a complete shit,' one of them said, which drew the riposte from the other: 'There is no need to be nice to him now he is dead.'

POLITICIANS ARE usually accused by the press of not being candid enough. Such an accusation could not be levelled against former Tory MP Sir John Foster – at any rate in private.

Once, he was being interviewed by Granada Television and gave a rather reactionary and patriotic response to their questions. After the interview was over, and the camera no longer recording, Sir John astounded the interviewer by saying: 'By the way, you ought to know that my public pronouncements bear no relation to my private views and there are three things I cannot stand – God, the Queen and the family.'

DURING THE 1960s, parliamentary debates were often enlivened by the young Northern Ireland MP Bernadette Devlin. Not so much by her speeches but by her unruly behaviour. On one occasion she strode across the floor of the House and struck Tory front-bencher Reginald Maudling several blows on the head. This and other antics led to Conservative MP Christopher Bland remarking: 'She should be ranked with the potato famine as one of Ireland's major natural catastrophes.'

LORD HAILSHAM has had an impressive career in politics serving under five Prime Ministers until his retirement in 1987.

Commenting on former Minister for War John Profumo, at the time of the Christine Keeler sex scandal, he was vitriolic: 'He lied and lied and lied. Lied to his friends, lied to his family, lied to his colleagues, lied to the House of Commons. A great party (the Conservative Party) is not to be brought down because of the squalid affair between a proven liar and a woman of easy virtue.'

And his view of high office: 'I've known all the recent Prime Ministers and not one of them died happy in his bed. Except Macmillan.'

Among his comments the following are worthy of note:

'One's convictions grow out of the seed and soil one's born in.'

'The only thing I know about economic rules is that there are no economic rules.'

'Most people who want to reform the legal system are grossly ignorant of the way it works, and so ignorant that they don't even realize how ignorant they are.'

On the bishops in the House of Lords: 'They treat everyone like patient peasants waiting to be told which way to vote. They don't understand that the Holy Spirit directs some people to be Socialists and some to be Conservatives.'

On a Conservative policy statement drafted by his Cabinet colleague R A Butler he did not disguise his disgust, saying: 'Your document is now as full of solecisms as a colander of holes, and as impregnated with bromides as a mothbáll with naphtha. I think it is past saving.'

NOT NORMALLY known for his insults, Lord Soper has occasionally silenced hecklers with a barbed reply. Once a man in his audience was ranting against Christianity and said: 'Christianity has been on the earth 2,000 years and look at the state of the world today.' To which Lord Soper replied: 'Water has been on the earth longer than that – and look at the colour of your neck.'

On another occasion, an aggressive character in a leather jacket shouted: 'What about reincarnation?' Soper replied: 'Well, the last thing I would want is to be reincarnated in an environment where I would encounter you all the time.' The heckler had the last word, bellowing back: 'Come off it. You said that in your last life.'

A FORMER Liberal leader got more than he bargained for from a member of the public during the second 1974 general election. Clad in oilskins, he emerged from a hovercraft declaring to a small group of holiday-makers 'I am Jeremy Thorpe.' He was silenced with the riposte: 'Well, that's your problem, not mine.'

LORD HAILSHAM on being Lord Chancellor: 'Sitting on the Woolsack in the House of Lords is very boring, so I used to sit there as little as possible and amused myself by saying "bollocks" to the Bishops.'

2
Educated Insolence

THE ONE class of person MPs do not usually insult is the constituent. However, even the most patient MP can occasionally lose his rag with a stubborn or just downright silly member of the public. One insulting response which has been used from time to time by a number of MPs is the reply: 'Dear Sir, Today I received an abusive letter from some crackpot who signed your name. I thought you should know about this as you may wish to take action to stop it.'

One MP used a slightly different tack. He once wrote: 'Dear Sir, My secretary, being a lady, cannot type what I think of you. I, being an honourable man, cannot write it, but you, being neither, will understand what I mean.'

Antony Henry, who was an MP at the beginning of the eighteenth century, was asked by a number of his constituents to vote against the Budget of 1714. Many current MPs envy his forthright reply. He wrote: 'Gentlemen, I have received your letter about the excise, and I am surprised at your insolence at writing to me at all. You know, and I know, that I bought this constituency. You know, and I know, that I am now determined to sell it, and you know what you think I don't know that you are now looking out for another buyer, and I know, what you certainly don't know, that I have now found another constituency to buy.'

He continued in a similar vein: 'About what you said about the excise, may God's curse light upon you all, and may it make your homes as open and as free to the excise officers as your wives and daughters have always been to me while I have represented your rascally constituency.'

The advent of universal suffrage and tabloid newspapers regrettably has destroyed such candour in our elected representatives.

As the franchise developed MPs began to moderate their response to criticisms from constituents. In 1774 Burke told his electors in Bristol, who demanded that he voted in a particular way, that he was not a mere delegate. His argument holds good today and ought to be printed in large type on the back of every polling card. He said: 'A constituent's wishes ought to have great weight with their MP. It is his duty to prefer their interests to his own. But his unbiased opinion, his mature judgement, his enlightened conscience, he ought not to sacrifice to you. Your representative owes you, not his industry only, but his judgement; and he betrays, instead of serving you, if he sacrifices it to your opinion ... government and legislation are matters of reason and judgement, and not of inclination.'

A MEMBER of Parliament like any other employer occasionally finds the need to dismiss staff. Some who see it coming leave of their own volition, just ahead of dismissal. One particular MP, who was delighted when an incompetent researcher finally moved on, provided the following reference: 'He has worked for me for over two years and when he left, I was completely satisfied.'

And, in a similar vein, another wrote: 'She has worked for me now for over six months, completely to her own satisfaction.'

THE HOUSE OF COMMONS lost an intellect of the highest calibre when veteran politician Enoch Powell was defeated in the 1987 general election. His notorious 'rivers of blood' speech over twenty years earlier has caused many to portray him unfairly as a one-issue right-wing bigot. Those who have served with him in Parliament do not subscribe to this one-dimensional grotesque caricature.

During his parliamentary career most of his problems were caused by an excess of honesty. When he was asked what he thought of a particular issue, he would reveal precisely what his thoughts were and not spare anyone's blushes. Such candour can be fatal to the aspirations of a democratic politician, as Powell discovered to his cost.

When a supporter told him that 'The world would be better with more people like you,' his response was typical. Most MPs would merely say: 'Thanks – I appreciate your support,' or some similar pleasantry and then walk on. Not Enoch. He replied: 'I disagree. A society for survival needs a spread of types. For example, in every battalion there's one man who deserves the VC, and one man who ought to be shot for cowardice. The battalion depends for its success upon a spectrum connecting those two. A country with everyone like me would be ungovernable.'

Commenting on a proposal for more EEC regulations he won wide support when he said: 'You don't have to live under the same laws as a foreigner in order to trade with him. You don't have to take the same kind of bath water.'

On Margaret Thatcher he observed: 'She is a very patient person. She can put up for a long time with being made to say what she doesn't believe. It's not exactly the mood of a person who is trapped – it's more the mood of a person who says "I don't like that. When I can settle accounts with that, I will settle accounts with it."'

During the early part of his government Labour premier Harold Wilson denied that he would ever use the bank rate for political purposes. Later, when the economic going got tough and he was obliged to do precisely this, he had to offer an explanation to the House. In a rather subdued manner and undoubtedly embarrassed by this volte-face, he made a statement on the matter and, not displaying any of his usual élan, he gabbled his statement at a hurried pace, keeping his head well down in his pile of notes. Amid a growing chorus of grunts and murmurs his speed appeared to accelerate. It seemed nothing could add to his discomfiture until the plaintiff tones of Enoch Powell were heard advising: 'Eat them slowly, Harold. Eat them slowly.'

Just before the 1987 election when Powell lost his seat, he was walking down a corridor and was greeted by Home Office Minister Peter Lloyd, who commented how well Enoch looked. Enoch scowled. 'Oh, it's come to that has it?' Baffled, the minister inquired: 'What do you mean?' 'There are three ages of man – youth, middle age and "oh, you are looking well",' he replied, before disappearing down the corridor.

FORMER LABOUR MP Ron Brown, who represented Edinburgh Leith until he was deselected by his own party, was always a colourful character. On one occasion when Margaret Thatcher, then Prime Minister, visited Edinburgh, Brown lunged towards her in what he later described as a 'protest about unemployment'. The Prime Minister was not injured but Brown faced court proceedings.

On another occasion when he was particularly unhappy about the turn of events in the Commons, he picked up the mace, removed it from its place and then hurled it across the floor of the chamber, causing much damage. On both occasions Brown's insults rebounded and he came off worse. Following the mace incident he was asked to apologize to the House, agreed to do so, but when he rose to his feet he started to try to justify his actions. As a result he lost the support of his own party, leading to a motion being proposed that he be suspended from the service of the House for twenty days and also be held responsible for the damage sustained to the mace. He further alienated his colleagues on that occasion by telling the House that if the mace was damaged he would find some unemployed engineering workers in Scotland to repair it, adding impertinently, 'If you are worried about a bauble Mr Speaker, then you are worried about nothing.'

SITTING QUIETLY before appearing on a radio show, Lord Jenkins of Hillhead was asked what he was thinking about. Insulting himself, he replied: 'I am just contemplating the vast expanses of my own ignorance.'

When he was Labour Home Secretary just prior to the second 1974 general election, he had some criticism of his own party, particularly of the robust line being taken by the then Industry Minister, Tony Benn. Jenkins sarcastically understated his complaint: 'Telling everybody who doesn't agree with you to go to hell is bound to alienate moderate opinion.'

Of former Chancellor Nigel Lawson he remarked: 'A manikin with a thick coating of bombast.'

🏛️

MARGARET (NOW LADY) THATCHER has never been afraid to express herself in the strongest possible terms. In the early days of her administration Mrs Thatcher held the view, correctly, that the majority of her Cabinet colleagues were 'wets' and did not share her beliefs. When someone alluded to a Cabinet rebellion she retorted: 'I am the Cabinet rebel.'

And putting in his place a colleague who questioned her approach she said: 'Do you think you would ever have heard of Christianity if the Apostles had gone out and said "I believe in consensus"?'

In 1992, commenting on the Labour Party's new-found enthusiasm for the EC, she snapped: 'When will Labour learn that you cannot build Jerusalem in Brussels?'

Among her other most memorable comments are:

'We are not in politics to ignore people's worries – we are in politics to deal with them.' Presumably she meant 'up to a point' because she had earlier made the contradictory remark: 'Many of our troubles are due to the fact that our people turn to politicians for everything.'

And giving her views on politicians generally: 'If you are

going to work for politicians, you should remember that they have very large fingers and very large toes and you can tread on them remarkably easily. I, however, have stubs!'

On the Labour government of Jim Callaghan: 'He presided over debt, drift and decay.'

Attacking left-wing television producers she remarked: 'Of course you have a duty to show the disfigurations of society as well as its more agreeable aspects. But if television in the western world uses its freedom continually to show all that is worst in our society, while the centrally controlled television of the Communist world, and the dictatorships, show only what is judged advantageous to them and suppress everything else – how are the uncommitted to judge between us? How can they fail to misjudge if they view matters only through a distorted mirror?'

And her view of the BBC: 'Over-committed, over-staffed and inefficient.'

On the now defunct SDP: 'They are people who hadn't the guts to fight when they were in the Labour Party. They put us under the thumb of the trade unions, they took us to the IMF – they are the self-same people.'

Taking a swipe at those who said she was 'an uncaring Prime Minister', she riposted: 'Some people just drool and drivel that they care. I turn round and say "Right, let's look to see what you actually do."'

She hit the mark when she observed: 'Being powerful is like being a lady. If you have to tell people you are, you aren't.'

And her view of the women's movement is terse: 'I owe nothing to women's lib.'

One political observer who was unimpressed with Mrs T's management of the British economy commented: 'She is the Enid Blyton of economics. Nothing must be allowed to spoil her simple plots.'

The journalist Peter Jay has described interviewing Margaret

Thatcher as 'Very like interviewing a telephone answering machine. You pose a question, you get an answer, and then you start to make a response and you find it's just going on and on and on.'

THROUGHOUT HER premiership Mrs Thatcher's right-hand man was Sir Geoffrey Howe. The former Deputy Prime Minister was in her team from the start and his resignation in 1990 delivered a mortal blow to her leadership. In his resignation statement, he criticized Mrs Thatcher's vision of Europe as a 'nightmare image' claiming that she looked out upon a continent 'that is positively teeming with ill-intentioned people, scheming, in her own words to "extinguish democracy", to "disown our national identities" and to lead us "through the back door into a federal Europe". What kind of vision is that?'

And he went on, devastatingly, to describe her habit of undermining colleagues saying her behaviour was 'like sending your opening batsmen to the crease only for them to find, the moment before the first balls are bowled, that their bats have been broken before the game by the team captain'. And he concluded a highly effective performance with the damning sentence: 'The time has come for others to consider their own response to the tragic conflict of loyalties with which I have myself wrestled for perhaps too long.'

During the same speech Howe took a swipe at the then Tory Party Chairman Kenneth Baker when he said: 'It has been suggested that I decided to resign solely because of questions of style and not on matters of substance. Indeed, if some of my former colleagues are to be believed, I must be the first minister in history who has resigned because he was in full agreement with government policy.'

The speech stunned the Commons and was regarded as

more damning than Leo Amery's diatribe against Neville Chamberlain in 1940.

🏛️

FORMER LABOUR LEADER Neil Kinnock deserves credit for releasing his party from the grip of Militant Tendency and bringing Labour close to winning the 1992 general election. But he had expected to do better and after two election defeats he wisely decided to throw in the towel as leader. Whilst he deserves praise for making Labour electable again, he cannot entirely escape the blame for the election defeats. His mercurial temper, his rambling loquacity and his premature triumphalism at Labour's Sheffield rally were all a big turn-off to the voters.

Despite being perceived by the public, probably correctly, as being totally unsuited for the role of PM, he is nevertheless usually worth listening to in the House. In debate he is sometimes effective but always colourful, with invective never far from the surface.

Pointing out that the 1992 general election was taking place during a recession, and that the Conservatives had already served three terms he said: 'If you had to ask a plumber not once, not twice, but three times to fix a leak, and you were standing in the kitchen up to your waist in water – would you call the same plumber to fix it again?'

On Norman (now Lord) Tebbit: 'He is like a boil on a verruca.'

On his party's former leader Harold (now Lord) Wilson: 'A petty bourgeois and he will remain so in spirit even if made a viscount.'

Alluding to John Major's campaigning style during the 1992 election he said: 'What's at issue in this election is not the soap boxes that Prime Ministers stand on. It's the cardboard boxes that people live in.'

On former Cabinet minister Kenneth Baker: 'He has been

described as being able to fall from grace without ever hitting the ground. He is adept at keeping one step ahead of his own debris. After being Secretary of State for Education he was appointed Chairman of the Conservative Party, thus proving that the Tory Party is one of the few organizations in which movement from education to propaganda is regarded as a promotion.'

Further commenting on the hapless Mr Baker: 'In making their choice (as to who should move and second the Royal Address in reply to the Queen's speech) the government Whips decided upon a mixture for that task. They decided upon a combination of exuberant and experienced, of smooth with rough, of loyal Heathite with loyal Thatcherite – and all of those qualities are conveniently gathered together in one person – Ken Baker.'

On Lord Joseph (formerly Sir Keith Joseph): 'He is the thinking man's Rhodes Boyson.'

And when asked precisely what he thought of Rhodes Boyson, he added: 'A man who thinks flowers grow by night.'

On former Education Minister Mark Carlisle: 'A wet now drying out – a mouse learning to become a rat.'

Mr Kinnock does not reserve his abuse only for Tories. On his former Shadow Cabinet colleague Michael Meacher he has said: 'He rushes around like a demented Santa Claus, scattering imaginary tenners from his sleigh.'

FORMER CHANCELLOR of the Exchequer Nigel (now Lord) Lawson was never a charismatic figure, nor someone who inspired with his oratory. He was, however, an intellectual heavyweight and a shrewd political operator, whose resignation was a severe blow to the Conservative government led by Margaret Thatcher.

His departure from active politics followed a number of disagreements with the then Prime Minister, culminating in a row over her appointment of Sir Alan Walters as her special economic advisor.

Following Nigel Lawson's resignation he has expounded on some of the traits of behaviour which he feels led to Mrs T's downfall: 'She had a growing tendency to dismiss or alienate her Thatcherite colleagues while retaining and promoting those who were opposed to everything she believed in. As time went by she saw her allies as political rivals to be cut down. She came increasingly to believe in her self-sufficiency and that she was the government and had no need of allies. There can be little doubt that these traits led to isolation and to her eventual downfall.'

On the way Mrs Thatcher handled foreign affairs he is vicious: 'I was frequently embarrassed by the way Margaret conducted herself within the European Community. Her tactics were counter-productive and damaging to the UK's interests. On most issues her approach was foolish. Her style and tone of voice came to irk the others (our EC partners) so much that they instinctively sank their differences and joined forces against her.'

And on her conduct of the government: 'She was, at all times, a politician and I was never entirely sure how much the saloon bar xenophobia of her later years represented her own uninhibited feelings and how far she saw it as a potential vote winner. Throughout her premiership, she had a fondness for seminars which were occasionally useful, but her unfortunate habit of playing to the gallery increased as the years went by. These seminars were characterized by an embarrassing tendency to abuse Geoffrey Howe in front of officials.'

And his view of the elements which brought down Margaret Thatcher: 'The row over ERM; the dawn of EMU; the poll tax; the prime ministerial ambitions of Michael Heseltine and the quasi-presidential aspirations of Margaret herself.'

His view of Prime Minister's question time: 'The questioning does not pretend to be a search for information.

But it does provide a continuous public examination of the character and competence of the Prime Minister of the day.'

His barbs on some of his contemporaries:

On Sir Geoffrey (now Lord) Howe: 'A fine mind and intellectual conviction more than made up for a somewhat colourless public personality and lack-lustre parliamentary performances.'

On former Cabinet minister Jim Prior: 'He was an affable but short-fused Heathite squire.'

On former Energy Secretary David Howell: 'He is, in Harold Macmillan's words, a gown-man and not a sword-man.'

On David Mellor: 'A brash, self-confident, ambitious and not over-sensitive lawyer.'

On former Chairman of the British Gas Corporation Denis Rooke: 'A large, craggy overbearing man. He treated ministers with a mixture of distrust, dislike and contempt.'

On former Cabinet colleague Kenneth Baker: 'Ken Baker's every instinct was to spend, spend, spend, a weakness mitigated only by the good humour with which he would normally retreat from the impossible position he initially adopted. He sought to secure his new status as a Cabinet minister by outdoing Margaret in his enthusiasm for the proposed new poll tax, clearly demonstrating his talent for presentation. It was only the policy that was wrong. He is a most civilized man with an agreeably sunny disposition, but not even his greatest friends would describe him as either a profound political thinker or a man with a mastery of detail. His instinctive answer to any problem is to throw glossy PR and large quantities of money at it, and his favoured brand of politics is the instant response to the cry of the moment.'

On former Foreign Secretary Francis Pym: 'A gloomy Heathite who has never been an admirer of Margaret That-cher. He was quite the gloomiest politician I have ever met.

He would dilate in the watches of the night on how democracy was doomed.'

On former Labour Leader John Smith: 'He is an effective parliamentary debater with a particular talent for mockery. His jokes are invariably better than his speeches, which are entirely predictable. He shows a reluctance to engage in serious economic argument.'

On Dennis Skinner MP: 'An austere left-wing xenophobe and conspiracy theorist – a maverick member with the best and quickest repartee in the House and a better sense of where the government was vulnerable than the whole of his party's front bench put together.'

On Donald Regan, the former United States Treasury Secretary: 'A silver-haired and sharp-suited former salesman. He was a rough diamond who cultivated a tough guy image and revelled in it. As a result, he was viewed with the utmost distaste by most of Washington.'

Of President Ronald Reagan he is complimentary: 'It is fashionable to mock Ronald Reagan, but I suspect that the verdict of history will be that he was America's most effective post-war President. His foreign policy stance, including the much derided 'star wars' project, undoubtedly hastened the collapse of Communism. He opposed the protectionist proposals that regularly emanated from Congress more bravely and more effectively than any other President.'

And his view of serving in government: 'The least important aspect of Cabinet membership, certainly in Margaret Thatcher's time, were the Cabinet meetings themselves. The Cabinet's customary role was to rubber stamp decisions that had already been taken. I used to look forward to Cabinet meetings as the most restful and relaxing event of the week!'

However, for those who urged Margaret Thatcher to make a u-turn he has no sympathy: 'What they offered was cold feet dressed up as high principle.'

MARGARET THATCHER ON DENIS HEALEY: 'Some Chancellors are micro-economic. Some Chancellors are fiscal. This one is just cheap.'

And attacking those who opposed the policy of privatization: 'No industry should remain under state ownership unless there is a positive and overwhelming case for it so doing. Inertia is not enough.'

When an American professor of politics observed to Lawson that ministerial life was far too busy to allow senior politicians any time to think, adding: 'What you need is a sabbatical,' Lawson replied: 'We do have sabbaticals in our system – we call it Opposition – and I've had enough of it.'

Of the Commonwealth he has never been an admirer: 'In political terms, it is a largely meaningless relic of empire – like the smile on the face of the Cheshire cat which remains when the cat has disappeared.'

On the position of Leader of the House of Commons: 'It is simply a second-rank job which provides no departmental power base at all.'

His view of British politics from 1979 to 1989, the period when he served as a minister: 'The Conservative Party was led by a team inspired by a coherent political philosophy and united under an outstanding leader – at the end it was undermined by that leader herself who regarded her team as dispensable and allowed the coherent philosophy to take second place to a cult of personality and personal infallibility. She became reckless over Europe, reckless over the poll tax, reckless over what she said in public and reckless over her colleagues.'

And on leaving office: 'The hardest part was not the trauma of my resignation. What I found unpleasant was the way in which I was made a scapegoat for all the ills with which the economy was afflicted.'

He has some justification for this comment. Following his resignation many pundits have sought to blame him for all our economic ills. Recently at Westminster one MP was overheard to remark: 'Lawson was a man who did to the economy what the Pope has never done to anyone.'

LEFT-WING LABOUR MP Tony Benn commenting on Michael Heseltine's tenure as President of the Board of Trade: 'He is presiding over loot and plunder of the public services in the interests of his grubby little business friends who financed his election success.' This led Mr Heseltine to reply: 'If the Labour Party talks the language it does, the most eloquent thing it can do is to bury its head in the sand.'

And bemoaning what he regards as a loss of power of the House of Commons, Benn has said: 'We are no longer even the primary source of debate as television has taken over. Mr Speaker Sissons and Mr Speaker Paxman presume to tell us what the nation should think.'

LABOUR'S ROY HATTERSLEY commenting on former Deputy Prime Minister Lord Whitelaw: 'All he does turns into farce, fiasco and failure. A representative of a dying Tory tradition – possession of land, enthusiasm for shooting small birds and antipathy for reading books.'

FORMER LABOUR front-bencher Denis Healey was a formidable Commons performer, his speeches being liberally laced with invective, ridicule and bile. He has recently taken a seat in the Upper House and it remains to be seen if his knock-about style is to the liking of their Lordships.

During his time as an MP his most frequent target for insult was Margaret Thatcher, whom he seemed to delight in attacking, usually in highly colourful language. He has described her as: 'The parrot on Ronald Reagan's shoulder', 'Winston Churchill in drag', 'Calamity Jane' and 'Bargain basement Boadicea'.

When the insult by the Russians, who called her the 'Iron Lady', was used by her admirers to point out her strength of character, Denis Healey quipped: 'She's got metal fatigue.'

And on the Conservative Party: 'Their Europeanism is nothing but Imperialism with an inferiority complex.'

[decorative portcullis symbol]

FORMER HOME SECRETARY Kenneth Baker is a polished Commons performer always worth listening to. Commenting on political journalists, he found considerable support from MPs for his gibe: 'They have no appetite for humble pie – even if it is served at their proprietor's cost in the best restaurants.'

On the lobby system whereby politicians pass on unattributable stories to political journalists: 'The political lobby consists of Members of Parliament who gossip to other Members of Parliament, who gossip to journalists, who gossip to other journalists, who then go back to their editors where they gossip again. Then they write their articles which are read by journalists and Members of Parliament as if they were written on tablets of stone. It is the most perfect system yet devised by man for the recycling of rubbish.'

On Labour's former Deputy Leader Roy Hattersley: 'There is an absence of decision in him and a daily struggle in his frame between sloth and indifference. He is a sour puss – there is no event that he attends on which he does not cast a blight.'

[decorative portcullis symbol]

THE QUIET and pleasant manner of Prime Minister John Major belies a shrewd and clever politician.

Shortly after he entered 10 Downing Street many articles appeared in the press highlighting his humble background. After a few days of press coverage of this sort, one rebellious Tory back-bencher was overheard to remark: 'I cannot stand his lowlier than thou attitude.'

A probably apocryphal story was told at Westminster in

December 1990, just after John Major entered number 10. It was said then that a Conservative MP was talking to a Russian diplomat who had once worked for the Russian secret service. The conversation turned to the subject of Britain's new Prime Minister and the Russian said: 'When John Major became Prime Minister, I looked him up in the KGB files ... and there was nothing there!' This supposed Russian comment was endorsed by a Labour MP who was heard to say of the Prime Minister: 'He rose without trace.'

John Major has never been afraid to 'mix it' at the dispatch box, and is a good Commons performer. Of politics generally, he has remarked: 'The person who never made a mistake is never a politician – and the person who admitted them to you wouldn't be a politician either.'

Commenting on former Labour Leader Michael Foot: 'His idea of a policy is to spend, spend, spend. He is the Viv Nicholson of politics.'

Taking a further swipe at Michael Foot: 'Whatever has gone wrong with the country in the past he blames on the Conservative government. I suspect if he caught measles he would claim that he caught it from the Treasury bench.'

Referring to Labour's so-called 'new industrial strategy' he said: 'Instead of a National Plan, Labour will now have a Medium-Term Industrial Strategy ... instead of George Brown, we shall have Gordon Brown – otherwise it is all the same.'

On Labour back-bencher Dennis Skinner: 'He frequently sees things as others cannot. If he had been at the walls of Jericho when they fell, he would have blamed the government for poor maintenance ... he needs a verbal straitjacket.'

And on Labour's spokesman Frank Dobson MP: 'He behaves like an agitated parrot with constipation. He is the best advertisement I have yet seen for televising the House. When people see how he behaves, they will realize he is more funny than he is wise.'

On Labour's policies for the 1992 election: 'It's Socialism – the massacre of the innocent by the ignorant.'

During the same election, commenting on Labour's talk of an electoral pact only a week before polling day, he remarked: 'What a show of confidence Labour have. One week before a general election they start cuddling up to the Liberals for support. Cuddling up to the Liberals is like leaning on candy floss.'

His description of the Labour Party's views on Europe: 'They have moved from total opposition to total sub-servience.'

On Neil Kinnock: 'If I had followed the advice of the Labour Party and of Neil Kinnock, we would be out of Europe, out of NATO, and out of respect. We would be living in an under-protected, over-taxed socialist backwater on the edge of Europe. Neil Kinnock has been wrong on every substantial issue in recent years. Once upon a time he wanted to tax the rich to help the poor – now he proposes to tax the rich and tax the poor.'

And replying to Mr Kinnock's challenge that the two party leaders should have a televised debate during the 1992 general election: 'We have better than a debate – we have a general election at which the case can be taken to the people. If I accurately recall my Shakespeare: "He draweth out the thread of his verbosity finer than the staple of his argument." Appropriately, that quote comes from *Love's Labour's Lost* – and Labour will lose.'

On Paddy Ashdown: 'He is a professional gloom-monger.'

On Norman (now Lord) Tebbit: 'He likes to bite your ankles even if you are not walking up his pathway.'

And taking a swipe at his critics, when a journalist asked him if he was about to change course, John Major retorted: 'I am not going to be distracted by froth and bubble – I am going to deal with the substantive issues in front of us.'

WHEN JOHN SMITH was elected Leader of the Labour Party, many Conservative MPs expressed their concern at his likely effectiveness. 'He looks and sounds like a provincial bank manager – and that is worrying,' one said, 'because unlike Neil Kinnock, he has a reassuring presence.'

However, only a few months later, following a poor showing during the summer of 1992, many Tories began referring to him as 'the Scottish undertaker', the implication being that his leadership was more likely to bury the Labour Party.

All we know for certain is that his premature death in 1994 robbed Labour of a formidable Commons debater who frequently used insult and humour to good effect.

During the world recession he gave his view of Norman Lamont: 'The Chancellor has the opposite of the Midas touch. Every area of the economy in which he predicts a recovery goes in the opposite direction. He has a non-Midas touch. It is no wonder that businesses cringe at the prospect of becoming the Chancellor's latest projected vehicle for recovery. They know that he is the personification of voodoo economics.'

And commenting on an assessment by the Chancellor of the Exchequer before the 1992 general election that the British economy was about to improve, Smith said: 'Norman Lamont's statements about the British economy are so absurd that they should be withdrawn and fed into the Treasury shredder – an overworked machine that is well used to pulping reams of bogus forecasts.'

On former Chancellor Nigel Lawson: 'He reminds me of the Emperor Nero, to whom he bears a passing facial resemblance. The difference is that Nero knew when Rome was burning.'

And contrasting Conservative Chancellors Nigel Lawson and Norman Lamont he remarked: 'Nigel Lawson, a former naval person, seemed to think that he was an aviator: we were treated to his notions of soft and hard landings. Unfortunately, he took some advice from the Opposition and left the plane rather hurriedly. Now we have a surfboarding Chancellor. In his mind's eye, he is a sort of bronzed figure in Bermuda shorts, riding the waves, taking on all-comers at the next Commonwealth Finance Ministers' conference. But is not the reality also revealed by that imagery? Surfboarders are not much in control of the essential elements; they are at the mercy of winds, waves and hidden currents. That is what is happening now. Norman Lamont is moving from wave to wave, not sure if he is heading for the beach or for the rocks and in perpetual danger of suffering what surfboarders call a "wipe-out". In his case, I suppose it is a major wipe-out.'

On the right-wing No Turning Back group: 'They make the Monday Club look like a sodden regiment.'

Commenting in 1988 on the relationship between Prime Minister Margaret Thatcher and her Chancellor of the Exchequer Nigel Lawson, before Lawson's resignation he said: 'We were told that there was no dispute and that they were both working in harmony. The truth is that an idiotic Punch and Judy show took place over who runs the shop. From what I read of interest rate policy this morning, it seems that Judy has slaughtered Punch. She may go on beating him and beating him again – because in the Punch and Judy show that is the present government, Judy always wins.'

And on Conservative back-bench MPs: 'If they showed just one glimmering of the sense of propriety that they exhibit in their own personal financial affairs, in respect of Britain's public financial affairs, we should make much more progress in this country.'

On John Major's government: 'This administration specializes not in creating real confidence, but in the peddling of worn out confidence tricks. Conservative policies have been an exercise in roller-coaster economics – the economics of boom and bust.'

And his view on the requirements of being a top politician: 'I don't think brains are terribly important in politics.'

🏛

FORMER CHANCELLOR OF THE EXCHEQUER Norman Lamont had two difficult years at the Treasury. Being in charge of the nation's finances during a world-wide recession meant that he was unfairly on the receiving end of more vitriol than the rest of the Cabinet put together. This has led many observers to overlook his own pugnacious output.

Following Neil Kinnock's 1992 election defeat and resignation, Lamont said of John Smith: 'As Oscar Wilde said, one would have needed a heart of stone not to laugh. After presenting his "shadow budget" it was in a mood of self-congratulation that he progressed to a Sheffield election rally to be anointed before an ecstatic crowd in a sort of mixture of Götterdämmerung and the Eurovision Song Contest. It was a short step from Budget Monday to Sheffield Wednesday and one more step towards Labour's calamity Thursday on election night. Any normal man might have been shaken by the election defeat, but not John Smith, who is nothing if not resourceful and resilient. Having failed to get the one job he had always wanted, he picked himself up from the floor and applied for another.'

Continuing to insult the then Labour leader he added: 'Those of us who know him well and who have listened to him often, know that he has one quality above all. He is extremely skilled at saying nothing. For months and years he came to this House and made speeches – brilliant speeches – to great acclaim, but in all that time, he never made the mistake of spoiling a good speech with a policy. Then the 1992 election came, and John Smith made one fatal error. Inexplicably, he lost his nerve and he actually set out a policy.

Admittedly, he did not go overboard. He set out only one, but that one policy was enough to lose Labour the election. It was a policy to increase taxes by £7 billion.'

Commenting on the leadership battle between Bryan Gould and John Smith: 'I have to sympathize with Bryan Gould. In order to make his leadership bid credible, he must explain why John Smith got Labour's tax plans wrong during the election and is not suitable to be leader of his party. But if he wants to be deputy leader, he also has to profess his undying support for John Smith and proclaim that he will serve him loyally as his deputy. This is a dilemma that calls for a brave face – or possibly even two.'

LABOUR'S SHADOW CHANCELLOR Gordon Brown is no slouch at the art of the parliamentary put-down. Commenting on John Major's administration: 'It is a government with no policy, a Cabinet with no leader, a Chancellor with no Exchequer and a Prime Minister with no ideas, no friends and soon no future.'

On the former Chancellor Norman Lamont: 'He describes a poetic image of the economy. He does not know when the recession will end, but pretends he does. Last May he said things were starting to go rather well and that "The green shoots of economic spring are appearing once again." It was a pure poetic image. It turned out not to be so much the "darling buds of May" as the "darling buds of May-be".'

He later added: 'The Chancellor has not just stopped supporting the pound. He has stopped supporting the Prime Minister, leaving him floating downwards to find his own level.'

On Michael Heseltine: 'He spent years in exile working out his plans. He promised so much. He stormed the country with his new ideas for an industrial strategy. He was the darling of the Conservative Associations, the hero of a thousand Conservative Party lunches. But the interventionist tiger of the rubber chicken circuit has now been brought low and reduced to trophy status. The tiger that was once the king of the jungle is now just the fireside rug – decorative and ostentatious, but essentially there to be walked all over.'

🏛️

LIBERAL DEMOCRAT leader Paddy Ashdown launched his party's new policy package in September 1992 calling it 'Challenge, Opportunity and Responsibility – a blueprint for future policies'. Surprisingly, this did not go down well with everyone. At the party conference only a week later, delegate Bernard Salmon said that Paddy's paper was 'woolly' and he went on to say that it should be renamed 'Fudge, Mudge, and Bollocks!'.

🏛️

TRADE AND INDUSTRY SECRETARY Michael Heseltine is a master of the political platform and anyone who interrupts him does so at their peril. His put-downs both in the House and on the platform can be devastating.

Recently he was speaking at a by-election meeting when a man in the audience wearing a large Labour rosette started protesting that the stewards were trying to make him remove his hat. He noisily resisted their attempts to make him sit down and refused to remove his titfer. Heseltine silenced him with 'I know why you don't want to take off your hat. It's because there's absolutely nothing underneath it!'

His view of former Labour leader Neil Kinnock: 'He is like a latter day Duke of York leading a one-legged army. Left, left, left, left...' He went on to describe Labour's election campaign as 'a three-week journey from red rose to red flag'.

And when John Smith succeeded Mr Kinnock: 'I always

knew Neil Kinnock belonged in the economic nursery, but now, God help us, we've got twins.'

On the late Labour MP Bob Cryer: 'He has his own obsessions but because they are peculiar to him, they have so little appeal outside the House.'

On Labour leader John Smith: 'He is a fence-sitter. If John Smith is the answer – what on earth can be the question?'

When the Labour Party decided to oppose a government motion on Europe Mr Heseltine referred to the U-turn with the barb: 'We were told that John Smith was a man of principle, but this is Harold Wilson at his worst. We now have a sort of "Harold Smith" leading the Labour Party. His policies are wall-to-wall whitewash.'

Rightly drawing attention to the fact that at the top of the Labour Party there are more Scots than Englishmen he referred to John Smith, Gordon Brown and Robin Cook as 'Scotland's revenge'.

On former Labour deputy leader Denis Healey: 'The trouble with Denis Healey is that he has all the intellect, all the experience and none of the integrity necessary for the job. He has become the worst sort of juke-box politician – he will play any tune that the occasion seems to demand.'

On former Labour back-bencher Martin Flannery: 'He has been dead from the neck up for years.'

And on his own career: 'I am humble enough to recognize that I have made mistakes, but politically astute enough to know that I have forgotten what they are.'

FORMER HERITAGE SECRETARY David Mellor was an extremely combative minister who would take on all-comers during his parliamentary performances. His resignation in 1992 over tabloid newspaper allegations about his private life robbed John Major of one of the most able members of his government.

However, nothing is certain in politics and Mellor may well return to the front bench at some time in the future.

Explaining his reason for resigning he did not mince his words when referring to his tormentors: 'These tabloid journalists have respected nothing and nobody, relentlessly pursuing relatives, friends and others and saying astonishingly offensive things. Maybe this is indeed the way the alternative criminal justice system, run by the media, should work, but I do question whether the greater public good is being served when one is entitled to bug, buy and abuse and use methods that are themselves amoral.'

During the 1992 general election campaign he evoked the film *The Silence of the Lambs* in a swipe at the then Labour leader: 'Hannibal Kinnock is the greatest serial spender in history. His politics will eat you alive.'

On Labour's policies of higher taxation: 'They proceed under a fundamentally false assumption. Taxation is a take-away, and reluctance to tax is not a give-away or a bribe. Their economic policy is a bit like a haggis – for most people it is okay, but only so long as they do not think too much about what has gone into it. Quite simply, Labour's tax plans do not convince. They would commend themselves only to the boxing promoter responsible for finding Mr Frank Bruno's next opponent, because they are guaranteed to stand up for not more than three minutes.'

On Labour leader John Smith: 'Some of the natives are getting restless with his supposed moderation, which is not delivering the goods. One minute he is monarch of the glens; the next some of his colleagues are itching for Scottish devolution, so that he can become an immigration officer on one of the less salubrious parts of Hadrian's Wall. The only support that the Labour Party is getting for its policies from City analysts is the support that the rope gives the hanged man.'

Mellor did surprise the Commons during one particular

speech when he appeared to give support to John Smith by claiming that the Labour leader was a supporter of the environment. 'John Smith is environmentally friendly,' he started, adding: 'Everything he says is recycled: we have heard it all before.'

Again on John Smith: 'Over the years he has got himself into more ludicrous positions than those in a Jane Fonda work-out.'

During a debate on taxation he twisted the knife into Labour's Treasury team calling them 'graduates of the Robert Maxwell School of Creative Accounting', adding: 'Labour are only too ready to ensure that public money is spent not once, not twice, but many times. I believe that in the Thames area water is consumed seven times before it reaches us here at Westminster. Similarly, Labour's taxes will be spent time and time again in the general election campaign as promise is overlaid by promise.'

Again on Labour's spending proposals: 'It is Dolly Parton economics – an incredible figure that would collapse without hidden support. It reminds me of the last will and testament of Rabelais who said "I owe much. I have nothing. The rest I leave to the poor."'

Replying to the gibe that the CBI would prefer a Labour government Mellor retorted: 'The CBI is about as anxious to have a Labour government as we would all be to have our daughters go to an all-night party at the Kennedys'.'

On a speech by a Labour MP on investment in British industry, Mellor retorted: 'We do not need any lectures from Labour on investment. It is rather like being lectured by Miss Elizabeth Taylor on the sanctity of marriage.'

On Gerald Kaufman: 'He sacrifices real depth for surface glitter – more like Richard Strauss than Bruckner.'

On Labour's Paul Boateng: 'It seems that his only function these days is to come into the chamber twice a day to laugh and to make animal noises. It is a sad deterioration in what was once a rather good career.' After this exchange Boateng interjected: 'We are waiting for a joke.' At this Mellor immediately offered to show the Labour MP a mirror.

On Labour back-bencher Peter Hain: 'The Peter Pan of student activists.'

To a heckler who attempted to disrupt one of his speeches he shot back: 'The gentleman is obviously well past his yell-by date.'

🏛

LABOUR'S FRONT-BENCH spokesman Frank Dobson is rather terse with his abuse. During a debate on finance he called David Mellor a 'pillock'. This caused Mr Mellor to respond: 'Frank Dobson has come alive again, like something out of the Hammer films that used to delight me as a child. He owes his facts to his imagination and his jokes to his memory. He is a member of the party which is making a rake's progress, moving from Robin Hood to robbin' everybody.'

🏛

SOCIAL SECURITY SECRETARY Peter Lilley has a quiet manner and is generally polite. Indeed, his cool, calm approach often makes an insult sound like a compliment! If you actually examine what he has said you realize that he is usually far from complimentary about his opponents.

On Labour's Gordon Brown: 'The Americans have a saying that an honest politician is one who, when he is bought, stays bought. With regard to the trade unions, Gordon Brown carries that to extremes. He stays bought even when he is being sold out. He carries integrity to the point of ineptitude.'

On Mr Brown's outlook: 'He overdoses on gloom. He cannot get enough of it. I fear that eventually it will consume him entirely and he will end up like one of those unfortunate old men in Oxford Street between the sandwich boards claiming "the end is nigh".'

On Labour's trade union policy: 'Everyone knows cosmetic changes simply do not do the trick. It is like putting lipstick on a bull terrier. What is underneath is still pretty ugly – and pretty vicious.'

Lilley taking a swipe at Michael Meacher: 'I have always admired his debating style. He is never knowingly understated. He is not afraid to exaggerate. He might even be described as the Dame Edna Everage of the Opposition front bench. Never in the field of public expenditure has so much been promised to so many at the expense of so few.'

▦

AFTER A particularly fierce debate between Messrs Brown and Lilley, Liberal Democrat spokesman Alex Carlile was moved to remark: 'During the debate my mind drifted to thinking about the difference between Dennis the Menace's dog Gnasha, and Lord Snooty and his pals. It strikes me that there is only one difference between those two caricatures: Gnasha uses maximum energy to minimum effect; Lord Snooty uses minimum energy to minimum effect. What we have just heard has sounded very much like that.'

And on Gordon Brown he added: 'He sounds like the Labour messenger who has forgotten to carry the message with him.'

▦

LABOUR BACK-BENCHER Austin Mitchell is a polished performer, although sometimes his television background takes over and his speeches begin to sound like a collection of sound bites from *The Comedians*.

On Peter Lilley he has remarked: 'He is like a petrified parrot.'

On the government's handling of the pit-closure programme: 'It takes enormous incompetence to make Arthur

MICHAEL HESELTINE ON JOHN SMITH, likening Labour's 1992 election campaign to the hit musical *Oliver*: 'His message to his party is "You've got to pick a pocket or two boys."'

Scargill look like a sensible, responsible statesman. John Major's government has managed it.'

Sometimes he may be long-winded, but no one can accuse Mr Mitchell of not being even-handed. He is often prepared to vent his invective against his own side as well as against the government.

His view of fellow Labour back-bencher Dennis Skinner: 'He turns being objectionable into a showbusiness gimmick.'

And at the time of John Smith's election as Labour Leader Mr Mitchell scarcely endeared himself to his new boss when he remarked: 'I decided to show my independence of mind by rebelling against party policies. Unfortunately, there are no policies to rebel against.'

He has gone on to say: 'Labour have become an HMV Party, parroting leadership lines we don't understand and can't now follow. The line has become a confused babble centring on "Don't blame the Germans" and "The Government is naughty for not behaving as stupidly as we would have done." We need to rethink ourselves back to the drawing board.'

FORMER EDUCATION SECRETARY John Patten has a bouncy and good-natured style. However, on occasions he has become irritated with Labour front-bencher Barry Sheerman, of whom he has said: 'I cannot understand what comes over him when he is in the chamber of the House of Commons. During debates in Committee, he is a hard-hitting, well-briefed debater. But once he gets on to the floor of the House something seems to happen. His colour changes, veins begin to throb and his eyes begin to bulge. I regret that he is Dr Jekyll in Committee and Mr Hyde in the chamber.'

Later he came to revise this opinion when, during the Committee stage of the Criminal Justice Bill in 1990, Labour's two Home Affairs spokesmen, the said Mr Sheerman and

Stuart Randall began to filibuster. This caused Mr Patten to dub the Labour team 'A couple of shellbacks – they are like two middle-aged mutant turtles.'

▦

Backbench Tory MP Peter Lloyd on Labour's former deputy leader Roy Hattersley: 'He has an imperfect grasp of what he is talking about, but he always has to fill his speeches with reports of famous victories. He likes to puff himself up like a bullfrog. He may impress some of his friends, but he looks risible to us.'

▦

OPPOSITION FRONT-BENCH spokesman Michael Meacher commenting on the appointment of Peter Lilley as Secretary of State for Social Security: 'One likes to think that the Prime Minister has a sense of humour in some of his appointments. On this occasion I fear that the joke may be at the expense of the unemployed.'

▦

CABINET MINISTER Michael Howard on Labour's Shadow Chancellor Gordon Brown: 'He is a happiness Hoover. The gloommonger in chief. When the story is grim, and the policies are dim, one knows that "It's got to be Gordon."'

On Neil Kinnock: 'As a pretender to the nation's driving seat, he has some notable qualifications. He loves reverse gear. His three-point turns are masterly. And, as for his principles, he never sets out without a complete set of spares.'

▦

FORMER LIBERAL LEADER Sir David Steel once silenced a heckler with the riposte: 'Of course I don't disagree with everything you say. Even a broken clock is right twice a day.'

LABOUR EMPLOYMENT spokesman John Prescott commenting on William Waldegrave being made Secretary of State for the Citizen's Charter: 'He has been described by the Prime Minister as the minister for little people – he seems more like the minister for paperclips to me.'

And his view on the Conservative policy of privatization: 'It is to do with kick-backs, greed and sleeze in the Tory Party.'

On the government's plans on rail privatization: 'This is not a Passenger's Charter. It is more a cherry-picker's charter – ripe for exploitation by property speculators, by route operators and by the Tories' City friends growing fat on commissions and fees resulting from the disposal of public assets.'

SIR NICHOLAS FAIRBAIRN is a first-rate lawyer and a colourful politician known among other things for his somewhat eccentric taste in clothes. He is often seen around the House wearing tartan trousers and unusual jackets, which he designs himself. He is extremely forthright in expressing his views and possesses a highly caustic tongue making it an extremely dangerous pastime to cross swords with this former Scottish law officer.

He frequently shocks his audience and appears to enjoy delivering barbed insults to friend and foe alike. In 1990, characteristically, he described his recreations in *Who's Who* as 'Growling, prowling, scowling and owling'. His 1993 *Who's Who* entry is even more colourful. He now lists his recreations as 'Drawing ships, making quips, confounding Whips and scuttling drips'.

When, during a recent speaking engagement at Edinburgh University a young female student had the temerity to mock his outfit, he retorted: 'You are a silly, rude bitch and since you are a potential breeder, God help the next generation.'

Asked about electoral law during the 1992 general election, he opined: 'Why should the bastard child of an American sailor serving in Dunoon have a vote in Scotland even though he's in America, when the legitimate son of a Gordon Highlander born in Daarnstadt who's resident in Carlisle has no vote or say in Scotland?'

A few years ago during a debate in Committee Sir Nicholas crossed swords with the former Labour MP, the late Norman Buchan. Mr Buchan was becoming quite excited during the debate on an amendment to the Criminal Justice Bill, arguing that no lawyer should in future have to wear a gown 'or a uniform of any kind'. Mr Buchan went somewhat over the top claiming that the purpose of all uniform and dress was merely to identify the office of the wearer. This was too much for Sir Nicholas who silenced him with: 'If that's what he thinks, why does the Honourable member wear trousers? Is it in order to have a crutch for his dignity – or to protect the dignity of his crutch?'

On Scottish Labour MP Dennis Canavan he remarked: 'I take the view that he, who knows more about madness than anyone else, should continue his career as a merchant of discourtesy elsewhere.'

He recently told a journalist: 'I was born the year that Hitler came to power, although he wasn't as good a painter as I am.'

On further European integration: 'Attempts to make Europe right and pure by being nice to those who want to divide it in their own interests won't work. All being called Schmidt and speaking Esperanto is not the way ahead.'

On John Major's Citizen's Charter: 'The concept's good, but it's wishy-washy and just another opportunity for bureaucratic officiousness.'

Although generally supporting John Major's government, Fairbairn does not like the Prime Minister's frequent references to 'a classless society'. Sir Nicholas has commented: 'What is it? Just a ridiculous phrase.'

Whilst he was serving as Solicitor-General for Scotland he was once asked by the Scottish Labour MP John Maxton if he appreciated that the 'alarming spread of glue sniffing among 14- and 15-year-olds is due to the lack of employment caused by his government and their consequent sense of uselessness', to which Nicholas Fairbairn replied: 'Glue sniffing is not a habit normally indulged in by children above the age of 16. It is a criminal offence to employ a child below that age. But if glue sniffing induces a sense of uselessness, it amazes me that the Honourable Member has not taken up the habit himself.'

In 1988 the salmonella crisis resulted in the resignation of Junior Health Minister Edwina Currie. Afterwards, during a routine debate Mr Fairbairn interrupted Edwina's speech with the barb: 'Does the Honourable Lady remember that she was an egg herself once; and very many members on all sides of this House regret that it was ever fertilized?' Vicious!

His view of marriage shocked many of his colleagues: 'Christian monogamy and its assumption of fidelity is as fallacious as the Catholic concept of the chastity of priests. I am sure that polygamy and harems probably worked better. We live in a priggish and prim age.'

And when asked what were the attractions (if any) of marriage he replied: 'Apart from the depth of the relationship, you remember when you turn over in bed who you're with – and you don't have to get up at dawn and get out.'

Upsetting in one swoop all women MPs he said: 'They don't give me feelings of femininity. They lack fragrance. They're definitely not desert island material. They all look as though they're from the 5th Kiev Stalinist machine-gun parade. As for Edwina Currie – well the only person who smells her fragrance is herself. I can't stand the hag.'

When fellow Tory MP Patrick Cormack attacked Sir Nicholas and referred to his 'eccentric and ridiculous utterances, bad manners and eccentric garb', Fairbairn said of Cormack: 'His manners are always appalling and his dress sense is worse. He is a squit.'

Sir Nicholas has had a long running line in insults against former Prime Minister Sir Edward Heath. This being so it came as quite a surprise when the press revealed that Sir Nicholas had sent a letter to Ted congratulating him on becoming a Knight of the Garter. Of this incident Fairbairn has said: 'The *Daily Telegraph* has said that while one could be rude to one's friends in private, one should be polite to them in public. Well that's the contrary to all I was brought up to believe. To write and rejoice in what was clearly for him a reason for great satisfaction for himself was the proper thing to do. But then, why can't I say he was a dreadful Prime Minister and his public behaviour is appalling? The fact that he sent my private letter to the press shows he has no manners. He has grave personality problems and torment within himself which he'll never resolve.'

And warming to this theme he said: 'To him chivalry is unknown. Since the Order of the Garter arose out of an incident in which man of little rank despised a lady of great standing, what could be more fitting?'

On fellow Tory William (now Lord) Whitelaw: 'He is the living person I most despise because he represents what I despise most – sanctimony, guile, false ingenuousness, slime and intrigue under a cloak of decency, for self-advancement – it's called hypocrisy.'

And on former Defence Minister Alan Clark: 'A rich goon with perverted views.'

After a particularly colourful insult by Sir Nicholas a Tory back-bench MP was overheard to remark: 'He is in his element again – hot water.'

LONDON LABOUR MP Tony Banks is highly articulate and amusing in debate and frequently peppers his contributions with invective.

He is an avid fan of the theatre, unlike Conservative back-bencher Terry Dicks, who is opposed to public subsidy of the arts, and about whom Mr Banks has said: 'He is an unreconstructed Member of Parliament. When he leaves the chamber, he probably goes to vandalize a few paintings somewhere. He is to the arts what Vlad the Impaler was to origami. He gives us a laugh.'

And warming to his criticism of Mr Dicks, his favourite *bête noire*: 'In arts debates, he plays the court jester. He has a muscular approach. He claims that the ballet is something for poofters in leotards. That is the level of his contribution. He is to the arts what the *Sun* is to English literature, or what the *A-Team* is to embroidery.'

Bemoaning the fact that some Labour MPs also have little enthusiasm for the arts he added: 'The Terry Dicks tendency is behind us as well as in front of us.'

During a debate on the advent of further television channels he winced: 'The thought of Edwina Currie coming at the public on ten different TV channels makes even the strongest man baulk.'

His views of some contemporary figures:

On former US President George Bush: 'He would not know a principle if it were stuck on the end of an Exocet and smashed straight through his head.'

On Margaret Thatcher: 'She is a half-mad old bag lady. The Finchley whinger. She said the poll tax was the government's flagship. Like a captain she went down with her flagship. Unfortunately for the Conservative Party, she keeps bobbing up again – her head keeps appearing above the waves.'

And expanding his views of Mrs T: 'She is about as environmentally friendly as the bubonic plague. I would be happy to see Margaret Thatcher stuffed, mounted, put in a glass case and left in a museum. She believes that anybody who opposes her – whether the Opposition or one of her friends – must by definition be wrong. She is a natural autocrat surrounded by a bunch of sycophants, many of whom have betrayed everything in which they once claimed to believe. She is far more influenced by the example of Attila the Hun than Sir Francis of Assisi. She is a petty-minded xenophobe who struts around the world interfering and lecturing in an arrogant and high-handed manner.'

Mr Banks on a Thatcher government reshuffle: 'She keeps changing her ministers around. They are like ducks at the fairground. We stand here and they keep coming round and no matter how much we pop them down, more keep popping up.'

On John Major: 'He has revealed himself as a Thatcherite with a grin. He deserves to be called Tinkerbell as all he has done is tinker with the problems of the British economy.'

On Chancellor Kenneth Clarke: 'In his usual arrogant and high-handed fashion, he dons his Thatcherite jackboots and stamps all over local opinion. He is like Hitler with a beer belly.'

On former Welsh Minister Nicholas Bennett: 'He has not actually practised sycophancy, because he is a natural sycophant.'

On Cranley Onslow MP: 'A fine example of a political thug.'

On Michael Heseltine: 'His contributions to debates are as if the House was not made up of Members of Parliament, but of delegates, all with their blue rinses and red necks applauding to the rafters, rather similar to when he makes one of his speeches to the Conservative Party conference.'

On former Food Minister Nicholas Soames: 'The amiable Crawley food mountain clearly likes his grub. At the despatch box he could probably persuade MPs that arsenic is quite palatable if suitably chilled.'

On former Transport Minister Peter Bottomley: 'So stupid and smug.'

On Nigel Lawson: 'Not the most lovable person. The news that he resigned gave me cause for concern. If he jumped from Number 11 Downing Street there would now be a very large hole in the road.'

On former Environment Secretary the late Nicholas Ridley: 'Brutal, graceless and almost a complete waste of space.'

On the Conservative government: 'There is very little which is decent in this government of second-hand car salesmen, Arthur Daleys and low life generally – on second thoughts, I have probably been unfair to second-hand car salesman.'

On the now defunct poll tax: 'It was a tax which was dreamt up by some half wit in the Department of the Environment. A tax which was unfair, unloved and unclear – a good description of Margaret Thatcher's government.'

During a defence debate he snapped: 'When Conservatives describe weapons of death and destruction they become positively orgasmic. Looking at them, those are probably the only orgasms that they are ever likely to have. Margaret Thatcher used to tremble with excitement at the thought of being able to press the nuclear button.'

On his own attitude to politics: 'I have always found it a great advantage to loathe my political opponents. It is not usually difficult, but John Major is not one of those that I loathe. How could I? We both grew up in Brixton. We both served as Lambeth councillors. We both like beans on toast. Where on this conjoined road of shared experiences did the Prime Minister go so badly wrong and become a Tory? I think that it was when he got turned down for the job of bus conductor. He had his heart set on punching tickets and helping little old ladies on and off the bus, but he was spurned. At that point he vowed hideous revenge on us all, but to be able to get it he first had to push a little old lady from Finchley off the bus. Having achieved that, he has now turned his attention to the rest of us. Our fate is to be even more horrible than to be frog-marched out of Downing Street. We are to be buried alive under charters. I thought that the Citizen's Charter was just one document, but there are more and more charters in store.'

When interrupted by Conservative gibes he airily brushed them aside with: 'It appears that we are in the midst of a convention of small order waiters.'

On the Young Conservatives: 'It is the Tory Party equivalent of the Hitler youth.'

On the state of Britain after 14 years of Conservative government: 'Britain is heading pell-mell towards the status of a banana monarchy but without the benefit of bananas. The Tories have deliberately created mass unemployment as a policy. It is their way of trying to break the powers of the trade union movement and of forcing wages down. What Victorian values mean to Conservatives is that many of them would be quite happy to see little boys once again earning pennies by going up chimneys.'

And his conclusion: 'There are times when I find it difficult to work out whether the Conservative government is vicious or ignorant. I have come to the conclusion that it is both.'

On the House of Commons: 'Words are cheap in the House. In some cases, they are almost useless.'

Sometimes Banks's sauce is too rich. When former Foreign Office Minister Tim Sainsbury was answering questions, Tony Banks bawled at him: 'Yankee lickspittle.' One MP who was hard of hearing thought Banks was ordering a type of cream cake sold in one of Mr Sainsbury's stores. However, the barb was unparliamentary and was heard by the Speaker who promptly ordered Mr Banks to withdraw.

Comparing the difference in speeches between Tony Benn and government minister Neil Hamilton, Banks commented: 'Comparing the two speeches is like comparing Demosthenes with Alf Garnett.' This led a government whip to shout: 'Which is which?'

His view of the gentlemen of the press: 'The average journalist was not at the front of the queue when brains were being handed out.'

However, not all of his colleagues are fans of Mr Banks. Fellow Labour MP Andrew Faulds has described some of his contributions as 'puerile comments from an inevitably loquacious colleague'.

Mr Faulds is not the only Socialist who has mixed feelings. During a rather lengthy speech Mr Banks expressed his disagreement with Tony Benn, who at the time was not in the chamber. Saying that he regarded Mr Benn's arguments as 'somewhat bankrupt' Mr Banks informed the House that he would ensure that his remarks were pointed out to Mr Benn 'as he probably does not spend a great deal of time reading my speeches – but then who does?' Which led Labour front-bencher Peter Snape to snipe: 'You do.' Displaying his knack of dispelling criticism from whatever quarter it emanates, Tony Banks responded: 'I most certainly do not bother to read my speeches because I know what a load of rubbish they are before anybody hears them.' No one in the House felt that they could argue with that!

Labour back-bencher Doug Hoyle was bemoaning the closure of British shipyards, arguing it would have been better if we had put the shipyards in mothballs. He then corrected himself and said that he would have preferred to have kept the shipyards open and instead put the then Trade and Industry Secretary, Peter Lilley, in mothballs. This led Tony Banks to gibe: 'They are the only balls he has.' Mr Hoyle agreed to bow to what he described as Mr Banks's 'superior knowledge of the minister's anatomy'.

During a debate on conservation in the Antarctic fellow Labour MP Peter Hardy pointed out that modern-day prospectors could do an enormous amount of damage in a small amount of time due to new technology. He illustrated his point by telling the House: 'Some people may imagine that a prospector is a hoary old man riding on a mule with a backpack of beans and dried bacon, hoping to extract a few bits of rocks with a hammer and a shovel and so discover gold.' At which point Tony Banks interrupted: 'This sounds like Nicholas Ridley.'

Banks added later: 'Britain still has the reputation of being the dirtiest nation in Europe. That must have something to do with the raw sewage contained in Nicholas Ridley's speeches.'

Commenting on John Major's performance on *Desert Island Discs*: 'He should have chosen something from *The Beggar's Opera* because there is a whole chorus on the London streets which could join in.'

FIERY LABOUR MP Dennis Skinner, widely known as the 'Beast of Bolsover', is a formidable opponent. He not only attends debates regularly and has one of the best voting records in the House, he is also adept at the art of throwing speakers off their stride by a well-placed interruption or comment.

When former Heritage Secretary David Mellor recently rose to speak he caused much laughter by shouting: 'Here comes swank.'

Similarly, when Margaret Thatcher was called to answer a debate, he interrupted: 'Here's the Westminster Ripper.'

In July 1992 he was rather basic in his abuse when he insulted the Agriculture Minister John Gummer, calling him 'this little squirt of a minister'. This criticism upset the Speaker, Betty Boothroyd, who ordered Mr Skinner to withdraw his remarks. He refused and was ordered to leave the chamber for the rest of that day's sitting.

Commenting on John Gummer later, he was unrepentant saying: 'He used to be the wart on Thatcher's nose.'

On Social Security Minister Peter Lilley: 'He's the baby-faced minister – the one with the Pampers on.'

He has recently taken to calling the Prime Minister a 'Ken Barlow replica', adding: 'We ought to get John Major a walk-on part in a re-run of *Crossroads*.'

On former Transport Minister Roger Freeman: 'A tin-pot minister who reckons to run the railways on Hornby-like tracks.'

Commenting on Tory MP Phillip Oppenheim: 'A millionaire mammy's boy.'

On the Conservative leadership election: 'They turned out Margaret Thatcher like a dog in the night.'

On the Conservative government: 'Tawdry and rotten'.

And on why Parliament keeps such odd hours: 'The biggest obstacle to changing hours – perhaps to 9 to 5 is the fact that more than 200 MPs – mainly Tory members – have moonlighting jobs, making money in the boardrooms and the law courts. They want to come to the House when it suits them.' This led to the response from Conservative David Harris: 'Dennis Skinner constantly talks rubbish. Most Conservative MPs work harder because we are members of committees. Dennis refuses to serve on them.' And Tory Patrick Nicholls added: 'It is unusual to see Dennis Skinner in the chamber out of prime television time.'

On the Liberal Democrats: 'All they are interested in is getting round Paddy Backdown – otherwise known as Captain Mainwaring – so that this little Dad's Army can have a caucus meeting to discuss what their policies are at the general election.'

During the 1992 general election, when it was revealed that Mr Ashdown had had an affair, Mr Skinner started referring to the leader of the Liberal Democrats as 'Paddy Pantsdown'.

His name for David (now Lord) Owen: 'Dr Death'.

On the press: 'In Britain, there is no such thing as a free press, as most of it is owned by a clique of millionaires.'

Occasionally during debate the person on the receiving end of the insult turns it back upon the perpetrator. But it is very rare for an insult to be thrown, improved and thrown back – only to be bettered by someone else, in a sort of verbal ping-pong-ping. Such an incident happened on the floor of the House on 16 January 1992 during Prime Minister's questions.

The only specialist knowledge that is required to gain the full flavour of the exchange is that in October 1990 Junior Minister Patrick Nicholls was forced to resign after being arrested on a drink-drive charge. He had foolishly decided to drive his own car after having an argument with a taxi driver over the proposed fare, which he refused to pay.

Questioning Prime Minister John Major on the rise in unemployment, the then Opposition leader Neil Kinnock called the PM a 'dodger'. Without batting an eyelid John Major, referring to the Opposition leader's failure to declare Labour's tax plans, retorted that Kinnock was a 'tax-dodger'. At this point Patrick Nicholls rose to ask the PM a supplementary question and this drew the sedentary retort from Mr Skinner, amid much laughter, (but unfortunately not heard by the press gallery): 'And here's the taxi-dodger.'

🏛

BRYAN GOULD was an extremely effective front-bench spokesman for Labour until he decided to resign from the shadow team over differences with his party's policy on Europe.

Commenting on former National Heritage Secretary David Mellor, before the resignation of both men: 'He is in government principally because of his ability to give a good-news gloss to any disaster that turns up. He is a man who would have hailed the sinking of the *Titanic* as a first in underwater exploration. He would have greeted the black death as a necessary step towards a leaner and fitter economy. He would

ROY HATTERSLEY ON DAVID OWEN AND DAVID STEEL during the SLD Alliance: 'They remind me of Hinge and Bracket.'

have celebrated the great fire of London as a vital contribution to urban regeneration.'

And on Cabinet minister Michael Portillo: 'One of the most bizarre aspects has been the transformation of his personality on becoming a Minister. When he began he was a man who was slightly austere, certainly rather detached and even commendably academic in style. Things changed when he changed his hairstyle to a sort of Heseltinian haystack. We then found that his eyes flashed, his lips curled, his nostrils flared and his voice vibrated with synthetic outrage. He gives all the appearance of having enrolled in a Youth Training Scheme leading to a diploma in the "Michael Heseltine School of Labour Bashing". Clearly, the qualifying test is the ability to spout absolute nonsense with utter conviction. The only point in which we can take comfort is that he shows no sign, so far, of reaching for the peroxide bottle.'

FORMER LABOUR front-bencher Gerald Kaufman has an acid tongue. After a loyal speech by Tim Smith MP, Mr Kaufman snapped: 'I knew he had learnt to speak but I did not know he had learnt to crawl.'

Commenting on Harold Wilson: 'He is the only man I know who deliberately acquired a sense of humour.'

On the Conservative Party: 'When the Tories think they are facing electoral defeat they dive head-first into the political sewer. The 1945 Gestapo scare has its equivalent in the 1992 scare that Saddam Hussein might take a risk or two. The Tory bogeymen may change, but the Tory's lack of principle remains the same.'

On Nigel Lawson: 'His style is a mixture of bluster, smugness and arrogance.'

Of Environment Minister John Selwyn Gummer, he said: 'A political pipsqueak'.

On John Major's government: 'They are particularly puny

and petty. They brandish their nuclear weapons like some macho symbol.'

And on the Prime Minister and his predecessor: 'The thing about Mrs Thatcher was there was a character to assassinate. The problem with Mr Major is that you look and look – and where is it?'

Recently Mr Kaufman has found himself somewhat unusually to be on the receiving end. Tory back-benchers have unkindly taken to calling him 'Kermit'.

TORY BACK-BENCHER Phillip Oppenheim MP on Gordon Brown MP: 'He does not deliver a speech, he delivers bile. However, we are entitled to ask, where is the beef?'

And Oppenheim on Neil Kinnock: 'He is an obscure Welsh politician, best known for losing his rag with Zimbabwean soldiers and for nutting people in public lavatories.'

But Labour's front-bench spokesman Donald Dewar has said of Mr O: 'He is the kind of person who gives a public school education a bad name.'

THE LATE LEFT-WING LABOUR MP Bob Cryer loved a verbal punch-up. When the front benches of the two main parties found themselves in agreement, Mr Cryer would do his best to wreck it. In his words. 'Consensus in the chamber is the worst aspect of Parliament at work.' He frequently put his views into action by dividing the House even when the official Opposition decided not to.

On politics: 'One of the problems of democracy is that we can never be sure of the outcome.'

And on the House of Commons he has said: 'One of the strengths of the Commons is that it is awkward.' It is fair to say that Mr Cryer, by his own definition, added to those strengths. He is missed on all sides of the House.

TORY MP and best-selling author Julian Critchley is always worth listening to in debate. His speeches are always witty and invariably peppered with insults.

On his own Party: 'Today the Conservative Party in the House of Commons contains the party conference of ten years ago. Cheerful girls in hats who once moved motions in favour of corporal and capital punishment on behalf of the Young Conservatives of some Midlands town, small-town solicitors and estate agents with flat provincial accents are now its members. As Mrs Thatcher went up in the world, so the Party came down.'

On Norman (now Lord) Tebbit: 'He was the rude child saying that the Emperor had no clothes. He didn't just say it – he shouted it from the roof tops. If he had entered politics a decade earlier, the Conservative Party would have been embarrassed by him but to the Thatcherites he was a hero. But he did not last long in government after the 1987 election. Like Dick Whittington, he turned again and made for the City.'

And commenting on Mr Tebbit's ennoblement: 'He should have taken the title "the Prince of Darkness".'

On tabloid columnist John Junor: 'That unamiable old Scot'.

Whilst on himself: 'I became a Tory not from conviction, but from pleasure.'

On former Labour leader Michael Foot: 'That distinguished old man of letters gave the impression of being no more at home in 1980s politics than Soames Forsyth would have been had he been dropped into a City office full of yuppies.'

On Neil Kinnock: 'Effective Opposition calls for a degree of subtlety and certainly for careful research to get the facts right. That was scarcely Neil's way. He was happier when getting to his feet, working himself into a peak of righteous indignation, and belting it out.'

On Jeffrey (now Lord) Archer: 'He was not a serious politician. But his footwork should command respect. He is proof of the proposition that in each of us lurks one bad novel.'

And on the late Robert Maxwell, who was once a Labour MP: 'Maxwell was the bad taste in the mouth but his zeal was unquestionable. The Bouncing Czech had resilience.'

'Public bar abuse is the stock-in-trade of the rougher end of the Labour Party.'

His view of government office: 'Junior ministers are chauffeur driven into obscurity, reappearing once a month at question time in order to read out replies prepared beforehand by some Wykehamist.'

On his long-time friend Michael Heseltine: 'He tends not to be able to see a parapet without ducking below it.'

During Mrs T's premiership he said of her: 'If she has a weakness it is for shopkeepers, which probably accounts for the fact that she cannot pass a branch of Marks and Spencer without inviting the manager to join her private office. In the party, the Military Cross has given way to Rotary Club badges. The Knights of the Shires have given way to estate agents and accountants.'

WHEN NORMAN (NOW LORD) TEBBIT is on form you cross swords with him in debate at your peril.

When asked who had the most influence on him, his mother or his father, he replied: 'I don't think either of them had. I think I had more influence on them.'

When a colleague suggested to Norman that he was probably someone who held the view that 'God was a paid-up member of the Conservative Party,' he replied: 'Yes, of course he is. God could not be a Socialist because of the process of evolution.' When asked to explain what he meant, he said: 'Evolution means getting rid of the dinosaurs and replacing them with some more efficient and up-to-date animals. Any Socialist would have been dedicated to protecting the dinosaurs in the name of compassion or conservation or something. The dinosaurs would never have been allowed to go. So God can't be a Socialist.'

On the Labour Party: 'It is a party full of envy, people with failures and richly tainted with smug hypocrisy. It shows malice towards personal success.'

On Neil Kinnock: 'More gimmicks than guts. I sometimes wonder whether he exists at all.'

On politics: 'A centrally controlled state leads to unpleasant consequences. Socialism is bound to become authoritarian.'

When he was told that Labour Cabinet ministers in office were at least well-meaning, he exploded: 'Well-intentioned and well-meaning people are the most dangerous. You cannot have Socialism unless you control incomes and prices. So you go the way of Hitler and Mussolini.'

'Anti-American talk is a sign of cheap and dirty parties seeking cheap and dirty votes.'

When he was told that he spent too much time trying to appease the party faithful, he shot back: 'The faithful won't vote for you unless you're faithful to them. I stand up for what I believe is right.'

COLUMNIST AND former MP Woodrow (now Lord) Wyatt on former premier Jim Callaghan: 'He was skilful in debate, persuasive in speech – and disastrous at his job.'

On politicians: 'A good character is not merely unnecessary for becoming Prime Minister – it may be positively harmful.'

On the House of Commons: 'The House listens with great humility to humbugs and compliments them on their sincerity. It hates to hear awkward truths and abuses those who tell them. It suffers fools, particularly sentimental ones, gladly.'

Former Liberal MP Cyril Smith commenting on Parliament

put it more succinctly: 'This place is the longest running farce in the West End.'

And: 'The consumption of alcohol does tend to encourage those MPs of all parties who can neither speak with effect nor be silent with dignity.'

GOVERNMENT WHIP and former Conservative Party vice-chairman Andrew Mitchell was once insulted by a senior Cabinet minister, but quite unintentionally. In 1987 he was standing for Parliament for the first time and just before the general election took place Chancellor Nigel Lawson attended a function to speak in his support. His constituents were astonished to be told by the Chancellor that they should 're-elect Andrew Mitchell because he has done such a good job in the House during the previous five years'. As a result, according to Mr Mitchell, his constituents have never believed a Cabinet minister since.

TORY BACK-BENCHER David Evans usually expresses himself in an extremely forthright manner.

On Britain's social security system and its claimants he is unequivocal: 'It caters for greed, not need. In Britain about 500,000 people who are unemployed have no intention whatsoever of working again. They blatantly milk the system, but have probably not missed an Oval test match or a set at Wimbledon for years. Forget Euro-Disney, London is the place to have fun – all at the expense of the British taxpayer. The mandatory sentence for those committing fraud should be a turn on the good ducking stool in the local river – a good public flogging would be even better.'

SCOTTISH LABOUR back-bencher Maria Fyfe commenting on

government minister, Michael Howard: 'He oozes insincerity from every pore. He strikes me as a man for whom the word "synthetic" would be a compliment because at least some synthetic things can be capable of useful service.'

FORMER ARTS MINISTER Tim Renton on Labour's Mark Fisher: 'He reminds me of the beautiful but sad words from *Macbeth*:

Life's but a walking shadow, a poor player,
That struts and frets his hour upon the stage,
And then is heard no more.

And he added: 'As he struts no more, he can take comfort from the fact that a new dinosaur gallery is opening in the Natural History Museum. I have no doubt that he will find himself one of the earliest acquisitions.'

On Labour back-bencher Tony Banks: 'When I went to the Young Vic recently, I was not certain whether Tony Banks would appear on the stage or in the audience. He is a natural actor.'

Dennis Skinner recently received a taste of his own medicine. When Mr Renton was the Arts and Libraries Minister, the Bolsover MP inquired of him: 'How many civil servants are (a) men or (b) women?' 'All of them,' came the reply.

THE WELSH Labour MP Paul Flynn taking a rather basic swipe at former National Heritage Secretary David Mellor said: 'When he loses his seat, he can get an alternative job delivering gorillagrams without the aid of a monkey suit.'

Mr Flynn seems to have something of a penchant for primate-related belligerence. Of the government's Welsh ministerial team he said: 'The three Welsh Office ministers have become the three unwise monkeys of Wales who neither see, hear, nor talk of unemployment, but hide from it. Are they three monkeys or three cheetahs?'

CABINET MINISTER Jonathan Aitken is an extremely polished performer, adept at the art of parliamentary insult. Commenting on Neil Kinnock he said: 'What staggers me about him is that when he chooses his weapons for a great debate, he picks boomerangs.'

After a lengthy speech by a Labour member, Aitken summed up the mood of MPs: 'Tony Lloyd anaesthetized the House with his own boredom. It was an amazing performance.'

Commenting on the first, and unsuccessful, challenge to Margaret Thatcher's leadership in 1989: 'I do not share the view that this is a great apocalyptic event. The charge by what may be called the light-in-the-head brigade will be led by that hitherto obscure equestrian animal, the stalking horse, now unmasked as my honourable friend the Kamikaze Sir Anthony Meyer. I have a message for him and his fellow horsemen. They have chosen the wrong time, the wrong battlefield and the wrong issue. It is wrong to confuse this manoeuvre with Europe and the EMS. All that stands for in their eyes is "Exit Maggie Soonest".'

On Labour's Defence spokesman Dr. John Reid, 'He has the air of a funny-money salesman about to perform a three-card trick. He talks pure statistical mumbo-jumbo and seeks to cover his embarrassment with a conjuror's handkerchief.'

SOMETIMES ONE can discomfit a colleague unintentionally. Former Pembroke MP and Welsh Minister Nicholas Bennett used to pack a punch during Welsh questions. Before he lost his seat in the 1992 general election he was renowned for his combative style.

On one occasion as he was entering the chamber for Welsh

questions, he asked me if I knew of any good insults which he might be able to use as he was expecting to be verbally assaulted by a group of Welsh Labour MPs. I flippantly replied: 'You could say that the trouble with the Welsh is that they ought to stop singing and get some coal up.'

During Welsh questions Bennett was not himself and although he turned in a fair performance, he was not as ebullient as usual. We met afterwards and I found out what was wrong. 'You bastard,' he said. 'That comment of yours stuck in my mind and I was so worried that I might blurt it out, I could not concentrate on anything else!'

About a year or so before he was defeated at the 1992 general election Mr Bennett was involved in an accident on a motorway when his car overturned. Miraculously he was not injured. Although there was no suggestion that the accident was his fault, one colleague quipped: 'Nick Bennett drives so fast that if a vehicle is not travelling at over 60 miles per hour, he thinks it's a house.'

Shortly after he lost his Pembroke seat in the 1992 general election Mr Bennett was at the House clearing his desk. As he was leaving he was approached by a member of the public who appeared to be lost and rather confused. 'Excuse me, sir, can you tell me how to get out of this building?' she asked Bennett. His reply was crisp: 'Certainly, madam. Stand as a Conservative candidate in Pembroke.'

SIR TEDDY TAYLOR recounting the flavour of his postbag said that when he decided to support the Wild Animals (Protection) Bill, which would have outlawed foxhunting, he received a letter from a constituent saying he was 'consorting with Communists', and another saying that he was 'supporting Socialist crackpots'. A further letter described him as 'a repulsive creep' – but he added, 'I didn't mind because I do not know what that is, but the most serious charge of all was the letter I had saying I was a "disgrace to the Monday Club".'

Following Britain's withdrawal from the ERM in 1992, a row developed between the British government and the German Bundesbank over a number of leaks that the latter made to the press concerning the value of the pound. The German government predictably defended the actions of the bank but this was too much for Mr Taylor who snapped: 'The German government is getting too big for their jackboots.'

THE GOVERNMENT Whips' office is the only department in government where the incumbents choose who is to be newly promoted to their number. In all other departments the choice is that of the Prime Minister, although the PM has a veto over the Whips' choice if he feels the person is unsuitable. The Whips make their choice by a 'blackball' system, whereby any one Whip can object to a person being admitted to the office.

Sydney Chapman, Vice-Chamberlain of Her Majesty's Household, is a senior member of the government Whips' office and a great raconteur. He likes telling the story, which may be apocryphal, of a particular MP who was rather over-ambitious and pushy. A rumour circulated that the said MP was about to be invited to join the Whips' office. To his colleagues' amazement the MP breezed in to the Smoking Room and started to order champagne all round. As each Whip entered, the MP would bellow out: 'Ah, here comes my *friend*.' He was therefore extremely disappointed when the official announcement the next day revealed that someone else had got the position. Taking the almost unprecedented step of trying to find out what had gone wrong, he approached one of the Whips and said: 'I had heard that I was to be the new Whip. Presumably I was blackballed because one of the Whips didn't like me. Tell me, who was it?' To which he

JOHN SMITH ON JOHN MAJOR: 'It has been the hallmark of Majorism to promise that good times are just around the corner. Unfortunately, we never turn the corner.'

received the reply: 'Well, I can't actually say how many blackballed you – but have you ever seen sheep shit?'

Mr Chapman was asked at a Rugby club dinner what he thought about Maastricht and replied: 'When I first heard the name, I thought it was something that gentlemen were not supposed to do to themselves.'

At one meeting in 1990 when the Conservatives were 20 points behind in the opinion polls, Mr Chapman was asked to describe his position in politics. He replied: 'A politician is someone who thinks only of the next election but a statesman is someone who thinks beyond that to the next generation. Ladies and gentlemen, standing before you you see a statesman ... In view of our party' standing in the polls at the present time, I just dare not think of the next election.'

Before the 1992 general election a back-bench MP (who is no longer in the House), a self-styled expert on the tactics of the IRA in Northern Ireland, was boring his colleagues with a long explanation of why IRA bombers behaved in a particular way. He referred to a recent terrorist attack and said: 'They actually meant to bomb M & S but instead they hit B & Q.' Mr Chapman ended the discussion with the barb: 'Perhaps the bombers were dyslexic.'

Former Whip Robert Hughes effectively silenced Labour back-bencher Eric Martlew a couple of years back when he told the House: 'He reminds me of one of those shredded wheat advertisements. He speaks bravely and beats his chest saying that he wants to debate an issue, but when it was suggested that the House might sit late, he starts whinging.'

A new Conservative MP, upon hearing that a colleague had been accused of corruption, asked a senior government Whip how he could be sure, when accepting a gift, that he was not breaking the House of Commons' rules. He was stunned by the reply. 'The guidelines are simple,' he was told. 'If you can eat it, drink it, or fuck it, it's not bribery.'

One senior Whip, when a debate was dragging on, accurately summed up the view of most MPs when he observed: 'If you speak after 10 o'clock at night, you don't win any arguments – you just lose friends.'

Before the collapse of the USSR, former Whip John Taylor MP had occasion to visit the Berlin Wall. He was amazed at the extent of graffiti daubed on this symbol of Eastern Bloc repression. He found himself scanning the scrawl to find something written in English, when his eyes lit upon the words 'Geoff Boycott – we love you'. He continued his trip and then returned to Britain where the following evening he was the guest speaker at a function organized by his local cricket club.

During the course of giving his views on world events he mentioned the very moving experience he had had visiting the Berlin Wall and added how he had searched the graffiti for some message written in English. He explained to them how the first intelligible sentence he had seen was 'Geoff Boycott – we love you'. On hearing this, some wag at the back of the room shouted out: 'Which side of the wall was it written on?' It was at that point that he felt he started to lose his audience.

Former Private Secretary to the Whips' office Sir Freddy Warren accurately described the behind-the-scenes art of the Whips' office when he commented: 'Whipping, like stripping, is best done in private.'

One Whip, seeing colleague David Davis MP at a wedding, remarked: 'What are you doing here – you're the funeral Whip.'

The motto of any government Whips' office: 'If you are nice – you lose.'

JUST AFTER he was elected to the House Tory Minister Jeremy Hanley was surprised to find himself sitting next to the Reverend Ian Paisley MP. Hanley remarked: 'I didn't know you were on our side,' to which he received the retort from Paisley: 'Never confuse sitting on your side with being on your side.'

🏛

BEFORE HE left the Commons in 1992 former Defence Minister Alan Clark was always worth listening to, as an insult or put-down was never far below the surface. Whilst a minister, he caused a furore by referring to one African state as 'Bongo Bongo land'.

On the media: 'The power of television has become fearsome and it is now being abused. TV is staffed by limousine liberals.'

When he was particularly rude towards Edwina Currie, Mrs C said: 'Oh, Alan, don't be so nasty,' to which he retorted: 'Ask around my dear. I am nasty.'

Widely known as a historian, when he was asked 'Where did you read history?', he snapped back: 'In an armchair.'

🏛

GOVERNMENT MINISTER Robert Atkins commenting on Labour's Dr Jeremy Bray: 'He behaves like a headless chicken.'

Shortly afterwards, a Tory back-bencher was heard to remark of Dr Bray: 'He is living proof that there is life after death.'

🏛

FORMER MINISTER the late Nicholas Ridley always had a sharp tongue. Commenting on Europe and the ERM in the inter-view which led to his resignation from the government, he said: 'This is all a German racket designed to take over the whole of Europe. It has to be thwarted. This rushed takeover by the Germans, with the French behaving like poodles to the Germans, is absolutely intolerable.' This led to the response by the former German Ambassador to London Karl von Hase: 'We appreciate frankness, but this is brutality.'

3
Across the Water

MANY OF the institutions of the United States of America are based on the British model. It is not surprising, therefore, that the USA having deliberately copied our democratic customs should find its elected members spending a similar amount of time trading insults.

Certainly the American public appear to hold their politicians in the same esteem. It was Mark Twain who wrote: 'Suppose you were an idiot and suppose you were a member of Congress – but I repeat myself.'

American humorist Will Rogers, a somewhat gentler observer, described politicians as 'a never-ending source of amusement, amazement and discouragement'. He went on to add: 'Congress has promised the country that it will adjourn next Tuesday. Let's hope we can depend on it. If they do, it will be the first promise they have kept.'

However, grumbles from the public, whinges from journalists and cracks from comedians all pale into insignificance compared with the vitriol politicians use against each other.

THE FIRST women to become members of Congress in the US were regarded as something of a curiosity. In the 1920s Speaker Longworth called them 'gentlewomen'. They were, however, subject to much teasing. On one occasion when a female member of Congress tried to intervene in a debate, she was dismissed by the congressman who held the floor with 'Not now – it's not often that a man is in a position to make a woman sit down and keep quiet.'

No one could keep Alice Roosevelt Longworth quiet for long. Commenting on politician Thomas Dewey in 1948 she inquired: 'Does a soufflé rise twice?'

And on Warren Harding she observed: 'He was not a bad man – he was just a slob.'

CLARE BOOTH LUCE was vitriolic about former US Governor George Wallace of whom she said: 'What he calls his global thinking, is, no matter how you slice it, still "globaloney".'

During the 1950s Republican Senator Wayne Morse decided to leave the Republican Party and join the Democrats. Clare Booth Luce silenced him with the barb: 'Whenever a Republican joins the Democrats, it raises the intelligence quotient of both parties.'

SENATOR SMOOT of Utah did not think much of British author D H Lawrence. Having read *Lady Chatterley's Lover*, he described Lawrence as 'a man with a soul so black that he would even obscure the darkness of hell'.

However, Smoot's aim to continue the ban on the book he regarded as obscene failed, causing another senator to remark: 'The United States has been officially lifted out of the infant class.'

DURING A particularly amusing debate in Congress, members of the public in the gallery started laughing so loud that it disrupted the proceedings. The presiding officer threatened to clear the galleries if the noise didn't cease, when Senator Barkley rose apparently to plead on behalf of the public, saying: 'I do not think that the Chair ought to be too hard on the galleries. When people go to a circus, they ought to be allowed to laugh at the monkey.'

This not only caused more laughter, but was quite a clever way of throwing an insult towards Senator Huey Long, who was speaking at the time.

DURING ONE particular debate, North Carolina's Senator Robert Reynolds who was known for his long-windedness was rambling on about the fascinating places he had visited around the world. The leader of the Senate, Mr Barkley, was anxious to conclude the business and sat there listening impatiently. Eventually Reynolds moved on to the beauties of the Far West and started describing the islands in the Pacific. At this point Barkley interrupted him and said: 'Senator, please, let us off when you get to Shanghai.'

On another occasion Senator Barkley was asked what made a wise Senator. He replied: 'To have good judgement. Good judgement comes from experience,' whereupon a student in the audience asked him what experience came from. Barkley's response: 'Well, that comes from bad judgement.'

OVER THE decades a number of congressmen have had a drinking problem. During one particularly boozy Congress where many of the elected representatives drank heavily, one politician posed a congressional riddle, namely; 'What is the difference between a discussion and a fight?'

The answer: 'Six bourbons.'

JENKIN LLOYD JONES gave some advice which many politicians today would do well to heed. On a political oration he said, 'It is a solemn responsibility. The man who makes a bad 30-minute speech to 200 people wastes only half an hour of his own time. But he wastes 100 hours of the audience's time – more than four days – which should be a hanging offence.'

IN 1811 Kentucky representative Henry Clay silenced Virginia congressman John Randolph who had said Clay wasn't paying any attention to his speeches. Clay shot back: 'You are mistaken. I will wager that I can repeat as many of your speeches as you can.' This silenced Randolph for the rest of the week.

IN THE 1830s American senator and lawyer Daniel Webster was an extremely effective orator who frequently used invective for effect. When a colleague named John Trout made an assertion which Webster did not believe, he started to refer to Trout as 'an amphibious animal'. After a while Trout became inquisitive and asked Webster precisely what he meant by this remark. Webster turned to his one-time friend and said: 'It means, John, an animal that lies equally well on land and on water.'

A Virginia senator called William Archer became the source of amusement to many of his colleagues for his preference for long-winded vocabulary. He was not a particularly good orator and for effect he used obscure, long words. The result of this was that his speeches were almost incomprehensible.

Daniel Webster's style was completely opposite, as he realized that a good orator had to be understood by even the slowest of audiences. A colleague from South Carolina called Preston one day asked Webster what he thought of Senator Archer. 'He's too fond of grandiloquence,' Webster said. 'What precisely do you mean?' Preston asked. 'Well, I dined with Archer today and I think he is a preposterous aggregation of heterogeneous paradoxes and perdurable peremptorences!'

ALEXANDER SMYTH was a long-winded bore. In the middle of one of his long speeches he noticed fellow congressman Henry Clay getting restless and said: 'You may speak for the present generation, but I speak for posterity.' To which Clay replied: 'Yes, and you seem resolved to continue speaking until your audience arrives.'

FORMER REPUBLICAN SENATOR Chauncey Depew, when challenged as to why he did not do more exercise, retorted: 'I get my exercise acting as a pall-bearer to my friends who exercise.'

One evening Depew found that he was due to speak at a dinner after the great wit Mark Twain. Twain spoke first and received a tremendous ovation when he sat down. Depew rose to his feet and said: 'Ladies and gentlemen, before this dinner Mark Twain and I made an agreement to trade speeches. He has just delivered my speech and I thank you for the pleasant manner in which you have received it. I regret to say that I have lost the notes of Mr Twain's speech and I cannot remember anything he had to say.' He then sat down.

IN 1894 Congressman O'Neill from Missouri was interrupted during a speech and he was so furious he snapped back: 'If the gall which you have in your heart could be poured into your stomach, you'd die instantly of the black vomit.'

FORMER SENATOR John Randolph who served Congress in the last century was a mudslinger. During one debate he called President John Quincy Adams 'a traitor', then he called Daniel Webster 'a vile slanderer', and referred to John Holmes as 'a dangerous fool'. He called another colleague 'the most contemptible and degraded of beings, who no man ought to touch, unless with a pair of tongs'.

However, Randolph did get his come-uppance. He had rather a high-pitched voice which caused Congressman Burges to snipe: 'He is impotent of everything but malevolence of purpose.'

Sometimes Randolph could be amusing. Of two congressional colleagues, Robert Wright and John Rae, he said: 'The House exhibits two anomalies – a Wright always wrong, and a Rae without light.'

And he called Mr Samuel Dexter, a politician who had shifted his views on a number of issues: 'Mr Ambi-Dexter'.

On power he said: 'Power alone can limit power.'

And on being in politics: 'It gives us that most delicious of all privileges – spending other people's money.'

He also said: 'Time is at once the most valuable and the most perishable of all our possessions.'

Randolph coined a number of *bons mots* amongst which the following are the most memorable:

'Asking the United States to surrender part of her sovereignty is like asking a lady to surrender part of her chastity.'

'We all have two educations – one which we receive from others and another – and the most valuable – which we give ourselves.'

FORMER MASSACHUSETTS Congressman Ben Butler was extremely long-winded and would usually fill his speeches with references to his military exploits during the American Civil War. This led to one of his colleagues saying: 'Every time Ben Butler opens his mouth, he puts his feats in it.'

OF COURSE some insults can be unintentional. Benjamin Tillman used to represent South Carolina in the Senate. His most striking distinguishing feature was that he had a very bad cast in his left eye. One day he asked a new Senate page boy the name of a recently elected senator sitting on the Republican side of the chamber. Unfortunately the page boy not only didn't know who the Republican senator was, he did not know Tillman either. The page boy left Tillman and went over to the Senate clerk and asked: 'Who is the man with one eye?' Without looking up, the clerk replied: 'Cyclops'. The page boy rushed back to Tillman and said: 'Now, Senator Cyclops, I will go and find out the other senator's name.' For once Tillman was speechless.

DEMOCRATIC SENATOR Henry Ashurst of Arizona didn't think much of his electorate. His attitude was: 'When I have to choose between voting for the people or for special interest groups, I always help the special interests. They remember. The people forget.'

FOR SHEER nerve former Republican Congressman Fred Schwegel must take the biscuit. The Iowa politician received many letters from his constituents on the subject of prohibition. The problem for Schwegel was that his electorate was equally divided on the issue. Whenever he was asked his views he would send out the following standard letter:

Dear Elector,

I had not intended to discuss this controversial subject at present. However, I want you to know that I do not run away from a controversy. I will take a stand on any issue at any time regardless of how controversial it may be. You have asked me how I feel about whisky and I will tell you.

If when you say 'whisky' you mean the devil's brew, the poison scourge, the bloody monster that defiles innocence, dethrones reason, destroys the home, creates misery and poverty, literally takes the bread from the mouths of little children; if you mean the evil drink that topples Christian men and women from the pinnacles of righteous, gracious living into the bottomless pit of degradation and despair, shame, helplessness and hopelessness – then certainly I am against it with all of my power.

But if, when you say 'whisky', you mean the oil of conversation, the philosophic wine, the ale that is consumed when good fellows get together, that puts a song in their hearts and laughter on their lips and the warm glow of contentment in their eyes; if you mean the drink that enables the man to magnify his joy and his happiness and to forget, if only for a little while, life's great tragedies, heartbreaks and sorrows; if you mean the drink the same which pours into our treasuries untold millions of dollars to provide tender care for our little crippled children, our blind, our deaf, our dumb, our aged and infirm, and allows us to build highways, hospitals and schools — then certainly, I am in favour of it.

This is my view and I will not compromise.

WHEN A man passed by with a pack of mules one southern congressman said to his northern colleague: 'There goes a number of your Minnesota constituents,' to which his colleague shot back: 'They must be going south to teach in your district school.'

DURING ONE particular election in Oklahoma Democratic Senator Robert Kerr was faced with a Republican opponent who was a preacher. They had agreed to a joint debate and the preacher went first, telling the audience, 'I became a candidate for the Senate only after I spent the night wrestling in prayer with the Lord and being told by Him that it was my duty to run for office.' When replying Kerr said: 'It is true that a senator holds a most important office and he can do much good for God and country. I can, therefore, concede of the possibility that the Almighty might urge an individual to run for the Senate.' He paused for a moment and then continued: 'It is inconceivable, however, that the Almighty would tell anyone to run for the Senate on the Republican ticket.' Kerr won the election.

AMERICAN POLITICAL campaigner Edgar Watson Howe coined a number of *bons mots* and the following are among his best:

'Some people never have anything except ideals.'

'He belongs to so many benevolent societies that he is destitute.'

'If you think before you speak, the other fellow gets in his joke first.'

'No man's credit is as good as his money.'

'One of the difficult tasks in this world is to convince a woman that even a bargain costs money.'

'The most natural man in a play is the villain.'

'Financial sense is knowing that certain men will promise to do certain things, and fail.'

'Express a mean opinion of yourself occasionally; it will show your friends that you know how to tell the truth.'

'A modest man is usually admired – if people ever hear of him.'

'Many a man is saved from being a thief by finding everything locked up.'

'The way out of trouble is never as simple as the way in.'

OHIO CONGRESSMAN Thomas Corwin was an effective orator in the 1840s. He was once cornered by a pompous colleague who began bragging about how he was a better orator than Corwin, and then started reciting long passages from some of the speeches he had given. The bore went on to say: 'If I didn't have so many irons in the fire, I'd publish every one of my speeches for posterity.' He got the response he deserved from Corwin: 'Take my advice, Senator, and put your speeches where your irons are.'

BEN BUTLER was a Republican candidate for Congress in the 1860s. During a political rally in New York he encountered much heckling which threatened to disrupt his speech. Suddenly an apple was thrown in his direction and hit him on

GEORGE BUSH on the American Congress: 'I extended
my hand to the congressional leaders – and they bit it.'

the head. Butler at once pulled out a knife and some of the people in the front row were frightened that he was going to start slashing out at some of the demonstrators near the stage. Instead, he bent over, picked up the apple, peeled it and began eating it. The crowd became quiet and Butler commented: 'Mmm, not a bad apple that.' He was cheered and then continued his speech in perfect silence.

AMERICAN PRESIDENT Abraham Lincoln, who was assassinated in 1865, is well known as a civil rights campaigner. However, he also had a barbed tongue. Of a colleague he remarked: 'He can compress the most words into the smallest idea better than any man I ever met.'

His view on slavery: 'What kills a skunk is the publicity it gives itself.'

And, in replying to an admirer who sent him a copy of a first edition, he gave the delightfully equivocal reply: 'Be sure that I shall lose no time in reading the book which you have sent me.'

In 1858 when Lincoln was standing for the Senate against Stephen Douglas, he said of his opponent: 'When I was a boy I spent considerable time sitting by the river. An old steam boat came by, the boiler of which was so small that when they blew the whistle, there wasn't enough steam to turn the paddle wheel. When the paddle wheel went around, they couldn't blow the whistle. My opponent, Mr Douglas, reminds me of that old steam boat, for it is evident that when he talks he can't think and when he thinks he can't talk.'

During that election Douglas and Lincoln held a number of debates in various parts of Illinois. During one of them Douglas made continual references to Lincoln's lowly origins, and in one particular speech he said that the first time he'd met Lincoln was across the counter of a general store where Lincoln was selling whisky. Realizing that there were temperance people in the audience, Douglas added: 'and he was an excellent bar tender too'. Thinking he'd got the better of his opponent, he sat down. Lincoln rose to his feet and capped Douglas's comments with this reply: 'What my opponent says is true. I did keep a general store and sometimes sold whisky. I particularly remember Mr Douglas as he was a very good customer. Many a time I have been on one side of the counter selling whisky to Mr Douglas who was on the other side. But now, here's the difference between us – I have left my side of the counter, but he sticks to his.'

Although he won the argument that night, Lincoln lost the election. When the result was declared, he said he felt 'like the boy who stubbed his toe. I am too big to cry, and too badly hurt to laugh.'

When his host mentioned a local historian and enthused: 'I doubt whether any man of our generation has plunged more deeply into the sacred fount of learning,' Lincoln, who was not impressed, snapped: 'Yes, or come up drier.'

Asked by a journalist who his grandfather was, he snapped back: 'I don't know who my grandfather was; I am much more concerned to know what his grandson will be.'

On one occasion he ignored a snide remark by a colleague and actually went out of his way to be polite. Later a friend asked why he had not dispatched the political foe and Lincoln explained: 'Am I not destroying an enemy when I make a friend of him?'

He later developed this philosophy further, adding: 'A drop of honey catches more flies than a gallon of gall. So with men. If you would win a man to your cause, first convince him that you are his sincere friend. Therein is a drop of honey which catches his heart, which, say what he will, is the high road to his reason.'

He did not think much of the refreshment provided on Capitol Hill. To one of the waiters he barked: 'If this is coffee, please bring me some tea; but if this is tea, please bring me some coffee.'

Of his electorate: 'It has been my experience that people who have no vices have very few virtues.'

On being accused of breaking an election pledge: 'Bad promises are better broken than kept.'

When he was asked to comment on the weight of his adversary Stephen Douglas's argument, he said: 'It is thin as the homeopathic soup that was made by boiling the shadow of a pigeon that had starved to death.'

On later being called a 'two-faced politician' by the said Mr Douglas, he replied: 'I leave the answer to my audience – if I had another face to wear, do you think I would wear this one?'

On a political colleague: 'He reminds me of the man who murdered both his parents and then, when sentence was about to be pronounced, pleaded for mercy on the grounds that he was an orphan.'

On being asked how long he held a grudge, he said: 'I choose always to make my statute of limitations a short one.'

On women: 'A woman is the only thing I am afraid of that I know will not hurt me.'

Asked what political tact was, he replied: 'The ability to describe others as they see themselves.'

Among his other sayings, the following are the best:

'No man has a good enough memory to make a successful liar.'

'I don't think much of a man who is not wiser today than he was yesterday.'

'I can make brigadier general in five minutes, but it is not easy to replace a hundred and ten horses.'

'The best thing about the future is that it comes only one day at a time.'

'Nearly all men can stand adversity, but if you want to test a man's character, give him power.'

His rebuttal of Socialism has stood the test of time, being frequently quoted to great effect by President Reagan in the 1980s: 'You cannot strengthen the weak by weakening the strong. You cannot help the wage earner by pulling down the wage payer. You cannot help the poor by destroying the rich. You cannot help men permanently by doing for them what they could and should do for themselves.'

When attacked for being a 'Conservative', he replied: 'Well, what is conservatism? Is it not adherence to the old and tried against the new and untried?'

DURING THE Civil War Pennsylvania Congressman Thaddeus Stevens said that he thought that the War Minister Simon Cameron was 'a consummate scoundrel'. When his friend queried what he meant, saying, 'Surely you don't think that Cameron would steal', Stevens thought about the matter and replied: 'Well, I don't think he would steal a red hot stove.' President Lincoln came to hear of the gibe, liked it, and repeated it himself on several occasions.

SOMETIMES AN insult can be used by a politician to get himself out of a highly embarrassing situation.

Once, when Washington Democratic Senator Henry Jackson was campaigning, he fell through a rotten stage floor and the audience started laughing at his predicament. He turned the situation to his advantage by quickly clambering back to the microphone and quipping: 'I was obviously standing on one of the planks from the Republican platform.'

IT IS NOT only bile and venom that over the years have threatened the good order of debate.

In the nineteenth century Massachusetts Senator Daniel Webster often imbibed too freely before making a speech. On one occasion he was in such a bad state as he was due to speak that a friend sitting behind him agreed to help him through the ordeal. As Webster stood wavering after his opening remarks, the senator sitting behind him whispered 'tariff'. It seemed to do the trick and Webster gathered his thoughts and proceeded to speak for a couple of minutes on the subject. Then he began to sway and nod. 'National debt' prompted his friend. Again, Webster was able to continue: 'Gentlemen, then there's the national debt – it should be paid.' At this point loud cheers broke out in the chamber which roused Webster. 'Yes, gentlemen,' he repeated himself. 'It should be paid.' This produced even louder cheers, at which point Webster seemed to have forgotten what he was talking about. 'And I'll be damned,' he said, taking out his cheque book, 'I'll pay it myself. How much is it?' At this, any bad temper that his drunken ramblings were arousing completely dissolved into loud laughter as Webster was always broke. He then collapsed into his chair and promptly fell asleep.

However, this amusing but rather disgraceful episode appears to have been the exception as far as Webster was concerned. Many contemporaries have commented that Webster was one of the few politicians who could speak effectively even when completely drunk. Indeed, many young politicians concluded that Webster did his best work 'whilst under the influence' and some of them drank to excess in the hope of becoming as fluent.

In Britain, F E Smith had a similar capacity, often amazing friends and colleagues with his witty speeches delivered when he was three sheets to the wind.

FORMER US PRESIDENT Thomas Jefferson was right on the

button when commenting about his office: 'No man will ever bring out of the Presidency the reputation which carries him into it.'

ONE-TIME Virginia Senator John Randolph was, in his day, one of the most striking figures to appear in Congress. He used to ride to Capitol Hill and enter the chamber with riding whip in hand and a small cap on his head. He was unpredictable – and usually very insulting.

On one occasion a man who had met him at a dinner a couple of days earlier saw him walking to the Capitol, rushed over to him and said: 'Good morning, Mr Randolph – how do you do?' 'Good morning,' Randolph replied without stopping or looking up. The man continued, 'You walk very fast, Mr Randolph, and I have great difficulty in keeping up with you.' Randolph snapped back: 'In that case, I'll increase the difficulty,' and he hurried off.

He was an ardent supporter of President Jefferson for most of his career, but he thought President John Quincy Adams was useless. He once met an Adams supporter on a narrow pavement. The man stopped in front of Randolph, completely blocking his way and said to him belligerently: 'I never step out of my way for puppies!' 'Oh, I always do,' said Randolph as he stepped aside. 'Please pass.'

In 1824 Henry Clay threw his support behind John Quincy Adams in the election of that year. After Adams's victory, he was made Secretary of State. Incensed, Randolph spoke of a 'corrupt bargain' between the two and, addressing the House in 1826, talked about 'the alliance – offensive and defensive' between the two men, later referring to their friendship as a deal between 'a puritan and a blackleg'. Clay deeply resented being called a blackleg, which meant a crooked gambler, and actually challenged Randolph to a duel. This incident, however, ended happily as when they fired their shots in the duel, both missed, and then made up their quarrel.

Towards the end of his life, he became somewhat senile, frequently tearing up his papers in sudden outbursts of anger. He directed that when he died he was to be buried facing west so he could keep an eye on Henry Clay whose nationalistic views he detested.

IN DECEMBER 1889 Maine's representative Thomas Reed became Speaker of the House and soon came to be respected for his forceful but firm rulings.

One day when his integrity was questioned by Richard Townsend, the congressman from Illinois, Reed announced to the House: 'There are only two sets of people whose opinions I respect. My constituents, who know me, and the House, which knows Townsend. It is hardly necessary to say, therefore, that I stand vindicated before both.'

Reed also showed that he had a sense of humour. He once sent a telegram to members of the House demanding their presence for a sitting as he was concerned to see that a quorum was achieved. One congressman who was held up by a flood which had washed away half of the railway line telegraphed back: 'Washout on the line. Can't come.' Reed immediately sent a telegram back: 'Buy a new shirt and come at once.'

When Reed was in conversation with one of the oldest congressmen in the House and he asked him to what he attributed his long life, the elderly politician replied: 'I always have a slug of liquor every afternoon and I vote a straight Democratic ticket.' Reed, who was a teetotaller, as well as being a fervent Republican replied: 'Well that explains it – one poison offsets the other.'

Among the most memorable of Speaker Reed's sayings are the following:

'A statesman is a politician who is dead.'

'All the wisdom of the world consists of shouting with the majority.'

Commenting on President Theodore Roosevelt he said: 'If there is one thing more than any other for which I admire him, it is his original discovery of the Ten Commandments.'

Of two fellow congressmen for whom he did not have a high opinion he said: 'They can never open their mouths without subtracting from the sum total of human knowledge.'

And, on a member of the opposition he said: 'The volume of his voice is equalled only by the volume of what he does not know.'

When William Springer, a Democrat, rose to his feet to ask for permission to make an apology for an incorrect attack he'd made on the Republican Party Reed exclaimed: 'No correction is needed – the House didn't believe you in the first place.'

On another occasion Congressman Lewis, who was rather good looking, raised a point of personal privilege when a tabloid newspaper referred to him as 'a thing of beauty and a joy forever'. Reed at first appeared to agree with him, saying it was a valid point, but then added, 'The newspaper should have said "a thing of beauty and a jaw forever".'

Commenting on the Senate: 'It is the little house – a close communion of old grannies and tabby cats. A place where good representatives go when they die.'

His view of those who specialize too much: 'If a man studies finance intimately, and continues his study long enough, it disqualifies him from talking intelligently upon any other subject. If he continues his studies still longer, it eventually disqualifies him from talking intelligently upon that!'

When Reed was campaigning in Maine during one presidential contest, a Democrat sat in the front row to heckle him. The Democrat kept asking impertinent and rude questions which Reed answered courteously.

It soon became obvious that the Democrat wanted to goad Reed into losing his temper, but Reed kept his cool. Finally, realizing that his ruse was not working, after a particularly polite and detailed answer to one of his questions, the heckler bawled: 'Oh, go to hell.' Reed immediately responded: 'I have travelled in many parts of the State and have spoken at many meetings, but this is the first time I have received an invitation to the Democratic headquarters.'

When a particular congressman who was in favour of war told Reed that it was the duty of the United States to 'take freedom to the Philippines', he shot back: 'Yes, canned freedom.'

ONE-TIME SENATOR OF UTAH, the Republican Reed Smoot used to tell of the incident when one of his pompous colleagues was in a Washington hotel being shaved by an old black barber who had seen many senators come and go through the years. The pompous politician said to the barber: 'You must have had many of my distinguished predecessors in your chair.'

'Yes,' answered the barber. 'I've known most of them and you remind me of Daniel Webster.'

The politician beamed with pride. 'Is it my profile or my speeches that remind you of him?' he inquired.

'Neither,' said the barber. 'It's your bad breath.'

CHURCH MINISTER Edward Hale became chaplain of the Senate in the United States in 1903. After he had been opening their sessions with a prayer for several weeks, a member of the public approached him in the street and said: 'Oh, I think I know you. Are you the man who prays for the senators?'

'No,' Dr Hale snapped. 'I am the man who looks at the senators and prays for the country.'

APPARENTLY, WHEN North Carolina Senator Robert Strange was on his death bed, he called for his son and said: 'On my tombstone I want the inscription "Here lies an honest Congressman".'

His son interjected: 'And then your name?'

'No,' said Strange, 'that won't be necessary. People who read it will say "That's strange!" '

IN 1919 President Wilson of the USA suffered a stroke. Senator Fall who had opposed some of Wilson's policies called to see him and said: 'Mr President, we have all been praying for you.' Wilson snapped: 'Ah, but which way?'

ALL GOOD orators have an off day. Senator Robert La Follette from Wisconsin, normally an excellent speaker, was making a speech in February 1912 to the Periodical Publishers Association and ignoring the late hour, he went on somewhat at length discussing the evils of corporate control of American newspapers. After he had been speaking for about an hour and a half on the same subject, he posed a rhetorical question to his audience and asked, 'Is there a way out?' At which some wag got to his feet, shouted, 'We hope so' and headed for the exit. Not only did this destroy the rest of La Follette's speech, but it effectively killed off his campaign for the Republican nomination for President that year!

Of course, not every time a member of the audience scores against the platform speaker is it intentional. At one political gathering Congressman Hancock of New York was due to address the audience at a meeting which started with some band music. After the orchestra had played a couple of numbers the chairman inadvertently insulted the guest speaker by asking: 'Do you want to speak now, or shall we let the audience enjoy themselves a little longer?'

Senator Claude Swanson of Virginia *was* deliberately insulted by an old dear in the audience after he had made a long and rambling speech. 'I liked your speech fine, Senator,' she said but then added, 'but it seems to me that you missed several excellent opportunities.' The senator was puzzled. 'Several opportunities for what?' he inquired. 'To quit,' she snapped.

LOUISIANA SENATOR Hughie Long, elected in 1930, was regarded as a formidable opponent. He compared Herbert Hoover to a 'hoot owl' and Franklin D Roosevelt to a 'scrootch owl'. Explaining himself, he said: 'A hoot owl bangs into the nest and knocks the hen clean off and catches her whilst she's falling. But a scrootch owl slips into the roost and scrootches up to the hen and talks softly to her. And then the hen just falls in love with him and the next thing you know, there ain't no hen.'

His name, Long, suited him. In 1935 he filibustered non-stop for fifteen and a half hours – one of the longest political speeches ever – against FDR's New Deal bill. During the course of his speech he read to the Senate the complete constitution of the United States, which caused satirist Will Rogers to quip: 'Most of the senators thought he was reviewing a new book.'

He hit the nail on the head when talking about effective political tactics: 'In a political fight, if there is nothing in favour of your own side, start a row in the opposition camp.'

Long aroused the ire of Senator Glass who, after one of Long's speeches, announced that Long's electorate had outdone Caligula. 'Where Caligula made his horse a consul, Long's constituents have made the posterior of a horse a US senator.'

Were he alive today, he would probably be suspended from the chamber for his bad language. With hindsight Long would probably have welcomed this to the alternative: on 8 September 1935, after making a particularly vicious speech, he was shot as he left the chamber. He died two days later.

US PRESIDENT Theodore Roosevelt who became President just after the turn of the century was a master of the political barb. He once called President Castro of Venezuela 'an unspeakably villainous little monkey'.

Of an American judge: 'He is an amiable old fuzzy-wuzzy with sweetbread brains.'

And he said of his successor Woodrow Wilson: 'He is a Byzantine logothete.'

On some demonstrators campaigning against blood sports: 'They are logical vegetarians of the flabbiest Hindoo type.'

Of William Jennings Bryan he said: 'He represents that type of farmer whose gate hangs on one hinge, whose old hat supplies the place of the missing window pane and who is more likely to be found at the crossroads grocery store than behind the plough.'

Roosevelt was also responsible for a number of new phrases entering the vocabulary. Among his many utterances he coined the sayings: 'the lunatic fringe', 'weazel words', and 'pussyfooting'.

FRANKLIN D ROOSEVELT said of his own career: 'I ask you to judge me by the enemies I have made.'

DURING THE 1940s Senator Wherry of Nebraska made quite a name for himself as a malapropist. In virtually every speech he would get something wrong. On one occasion he referred to 'Indigo China'. He later called the Chinese Nationalist leader Chiang Kai-Shek 'Shanghai Jack'. He once said: 'The issue is clear and indistinct to me.' And speaking of the defence department joint chiefs of staff he alluded to 'the chief joints of staff'. However, those he insulted knew that he couldn't help it and he came to be affectionately known as 'the Sam Goldwyn of Capitol Hill'.

TEXAS REPRESENTATIVE Sam Rayburn became Speaker of the House of Representatives in 1940. He prided himself in telling the truth as he saw it, even if this meant upsetting his friends. His local preacher criticized Rayburn's support for President Truman's sacking of General MacArthur and added: 'If your constituents elect you to office again, they will be deaf, dumb and ignorant.' Rayburn turned to the preacher and said: 'Being a believer in God and his word, which was "and on earth, peace and goodwill to all men", I fear that your conduct will not be conducive to carrying out these things. In other words, God travelling with you would be in poor company,' and then he walked off.

Among his many quips, insults and sayings the following are the best:

'Any man who becomes conceited and arrogant isn't big enough for the job.'

'Anyone who will cheat for you, will cheat against you.'

'There is a time to fish and a time to mend nets.'

'If there is anything I hate more than an old fogey, it's a young fogey.'

'No one has a finer command of language than the person who keeps his mouth shut.'

'Always tell the truth then you'll never have to remember what you said the last time.'

He snapped back at a critic who didn't think he was being partisan enough: 'Remember, number one: we're Americans first and Democrats second. And number two: we're builders not obstructionists. Any jackass can kick down the barn door, but it takes a carpenter to build one.'

And taking a swipe at a colleague who criticized the United States overseas: 'Politics should stop at the water's edge – when it comes to foreign policy you support your country.'

DURING 1939 on the eve of the Second World War, the British King and Queen visited Washington to secure further help from the US towards Britain's war effort.

The royal family were insulted – though not intentionally – by the behaviour of Congressman Joe Martin. He was a member of the committee deputed to welcome the royal couple and, like the other committee members, he was expected to wear a morning coat and silk top hat for the occasion.

The day before the trip Texas Congressman Sam Rayburn told Joe Martin that he didn't have a top hat and wasn't going to get one. He indicated that he was just going to wear a bowler hat. Martin did have a top hat, but since Rayburn didn't, he decided to give moral support to his old friend and wear his bowler hat also.

When he got to Capitol Hill the next day, however, he was amazed to find Rayburn wearing a shiny silk hat which someone had lent him at the last minute.

Martin had no alternative but to attend the reception wearing his bowler hat whilst everyone else was properly attired. Local newspapers made much of the 'snub' and there was considerable criticism from other congressmen.

Whether or not the royal couple noticed is not recorded, but clearly Martin's colleagues and the press thought it was a deliberate insult. Worried about the reaction of his constituents, in view of all of the publicity, Martin was amazed to find that on his return to Massachusetts he was regarded as a hero. Constituency mail poured into his office praising his 'plucky performance'. Local party workers patted him on the back and said they were glad that he had the gumption to stand up to the King of England rather than crawl to him in a high hat as others had done.

Which all goes to show that in politics, public reaction is always unpredictable.

PAT HARRISON, a Mississippi senator, did not have much time for Theodore Bilbo, a senator from the same State, of whom he said: 'When Bilbo dies the epitaph on his gravestone should read: "Here lies Bilbo, deep in the dirt he loved so well."'

ONCE WHEN John Allen of Mississippi was standing for Congress, he agreed to a debate with his opponent one W B Walker. Walker spoke first and said to the audience: 'Ladies and gentlemen, I want you to notice my opponent Mr Allen. Just look at him sitting over there, big and fat. He's literally pregnant on other people's money, he has been in Congress so long.' When Allen's time came to speak he patted his large stomach and said: 'What Mr Walker said is true about me being pregnant. If it's a girl I will name it Martha Washington. If it's a boy, I will name it George Washington, and if it's a jackass, I will name it W B Walker.'

FOR THE candidates, most election campaigns have their difficulties. The reason is simple. It is impossible for a politician to express his opinion on the issues of the day without alienating some of his voters. The most successful constituency members are those who never talk politics in their own area, but confine themselves to issues where there is a broad consensus – such as improving the road network in the area, having the pavements resurfaced or campaigning for increased pensions. However, the general election public meeting is one occasion when a politician cannot avoid controversy, quite simply because he is certain to be asked a question on a current contentious issue. Texas Senator Tom Connally had a deft way of deflecting these questions. Once when he was in east Texas he was addressing an open-air crowd and his speech went down quite well. He was then asked a question by a farmer in the audience who said: 'How do you stand on the cotton issue?' Without a moment's hesitation Connally replied: 'I am OK on that one. Are there any other questions?'

AMERICAN PRESIDENT Calvin Coolidge effectively pleaded the cause for political inaction when he said: 'In politics, if you see ten troubles coming down the road, you can be sure that nine of them will run into the ditch before they reach you.'

DURING A rambling and almost incoherent speech made by a colleague in the Senate, Senator Eugene Millikin interrupted with: 'If the distinguished senator will allow me, I will try to extricate him from his thoughts.'

TAKING THE blame for an unfortunate decision by a sub-ordinate, former American President Harry S Truman coined the phrase: 'The buck stops here.'

On trying to control children: 'I have found that the best way to give advice to your children is to find out what they want and then advise them to do it.'

On himself: 'I am not sure that I managed it, but I did learn that a great leader is a man who has the ability to get other people to do what they don't want to do – and like it.'

And insulting himself: 'Well, my speech seems to have been a hit according to all the newspapers. It shows you never can tell. I thought it was rotten.'

Among his other comments, the following are worthy of note:

'Don't talk about rope in the house of somebody who has been hanged.'

'Whenever an elector tells me he's non-partisan, I know that he's going to vote against me.'

'Statesmen are more expendable than soldiers.'

And slapping down a journalist who was commenting about Truman's poor family background: 'My father was not a failure. After all, he was the father of a President of the United States.'

To another journalist he barked: 'If you want to ask me an impudent question, that's all right. I will give you an impudent answer.'

On Richard Nixon's first attempt to become President: 'You don't send a fox to watch the chickens just because he has had a lot of experience in the hen house.'

Towards the end of the war he said: 'If we see that Germany is winning the war, we ought to help Russia, and if Russia is winning, we ought to help Germany, and in that way let them kill as many as possible.'

Truman commenting on his successor: 'Some of the newspapers are making snide remarks about Mrs Eisenhower saying she has a drinking problem. It wouldn't surprise me if she did because look what that poor woman has to put up with. She's married to a no-good son of a bitch.'

▲

FAMOUS AMERICAN cartoonist Al Capp, who created the character Li'l Abner, was attending a party when he was introduced by the hostess to President Truman 'Mr President, I'd like you to meet the famous comic strip cartoonist, Al Capp,' to which the President inquired: 'Which comic strip?' The hostess turned to Mr Capp and said to him: 'I'd like to introduce you to President Truman,' to which Capp quipped back: 'Which country?'

FORMER KENTUCKY SENATOR Alben Barkley, who was Harry Truman's vice-president, had been happily married for many years when he was asked what his formula was for a successful marriage. He replied: 'My wife and I have an agreement that she makes all the small decisions and I make all the big ones.' 'And have you ever argued?' a journalist asked. 'Never,' he replied, later adding: 'But then, we have never had to make a big decision.'

The Chairman of the Aluminium Association of America was not a Barkley fan and he found an effective way of deflating the vice-president after Barkley had made a prepared speech to the Association. Barkley thought he had done quite well but the Chairman rose from his seat and told the audience: 'I have three criticisms. In the first place, you read your speech. In the second place, you read it poorly. And in the third place, it wasn't worth reading,' before disappearing out of the door.

FAILED AMERICAN presidential candidate Adlai Stevenson was a great wit, but suffered from the fact that he was not 'televisual'. In some respects, as a presidential candidate he was the complete opposite of Ronald Reagan. Although his televised interviews made a poor impression, he had a sharp and crackling wit and was not afraid to speak his mind.

The following are among his most memorable quotes:

'A lie is an abomination unto the Lord – and a very pleasant help in time of trouble.'

'A hungry man is not a free man.'

'A free society is one where it is safe to be unpopular.'

'Flattery is all right – if you don't inhale.'

Stevenson also said: 'The human race has improved everything except the human race.'

Adapting the saying by Lord Acton (it was Acton who said, 'Power tends to corrupt and absolute power corrupts absolutely'), he said: 'Power corrupts, but lack of power corrupts absolutely.'

REPUBLICAN PRESIDENTIAL CANDIDATE Barry Goldwater was regarded by the majority of Americans as unelectable because of his extremist views. However, he did have the ability to encapsulate his arguments succinctly. He said: 'Minority groups now speak much more loudly than do majority groups which I classify as the forgotten American ... the man who pays his taxes, prays, behaves himself, stays out of trouble and works for his government.'

During the early 1960s Goldwater often came into confrontation with Liberal Senator Hubert Humphrey. Humphrey regarded Goldwater with some justification as extremely right-wing and reactionary. When they met at a reception given in Hollywood for a movie company, Humphrey said: 'Senator Goldwater would have been a great success in the movies – working for 18th Century Fox.'

Goldwater, however, got his own back. Of Humphrey he remarked: 'He talks so fast that listening to him is like trying to read *Playboy* magazine with your wife turning the pages.'

HUBERT HUMPHREY is perhaps better remembered not as a senator but as a failed presidential candidate. After his own ambitions to enter the White House had been destroyed, he gave some good advice to losers: 'If you can't cry a bit in politics, the only other thing you'll have is hate.'

FORMER US GOVERNOR George Wallace often gave the impression that he thrived on hate. When asked by the press how he would react to demonstrators blocking his way he snapped back: 'If any demonstrator lies down in front of my car – it will be the last car he will ever lie down in front of.'

AMERICAN ROBERT JACKSON accurately summed up one of the problems of a democracy: 'The price of freedom of religion or of speech or of the press is that we must put up with, and even pay for, a good deal of rubbish.'

FORMER DEMOCRATIC PRESIDENT Lyndon Johnson did not think much of Jack Kennedy before Kennedy became President, saying of him: 'He's just a flash in the pan. The boy has no record of substance.'

And of former Kennedy aide Bob Griffin he thought even less: 'He's not going anywhere. That elongated son of a bitch looks down his nose at me like I'm shit. Every time I see him I almost go through the roof.'

In 1948 before Johnson had aspirations to become President, he stood for election to the United States Senate. He won, but by such a narrow margin that some of his opponents alleged that he had rigged the ballot. They referred to him sarcastically as 'Landslide Lyndon'.

These allegations led some Republicans to tell the story of a man who came across a small Mexican boy who was crying his heart out. 'Why are you crying?' asked the man. The Mexican lad replied, 'My daddy doesn't love me.' The man was rather amazed by this response as he knew that the boy's father had been dead for some time. 'But your daddy is dead,' the man replied. 'Yes,' cried the lad, 'but he came back to vote for Lyndon Johnson and he didn't come to see me.'

Of President Gerald Ford Johnson remarked: 'He is a nice guy, but he played too much football with his helmet off.'

His advice on when to trust colleagues: 'I never trust a man unless I've got his pecker in my pocket.'

His definition of foreigners: 'They ain't like the folk you were reared with.'

On conquest: 'The best fertilizer for a piece of land is the footprints of its owner.'

JAMES MICHAEL CURLEY, four times Mayor of Boston in the United States, was something of a rascal who didn't mind bending the rules to get his own way. His motto used to be: 'Do unto others as they wish to do unto you – but do it first.' One opponent whom Curley did it to first started to refer to him as 'old cabbage ears', and the name stuck.

His methods were unorthodox, but usually effective. Once when his office was owed a large amount of money, he realized that he was unable to pay all of the city employees on time. He personally telephoned the chairman of the company who owed the debt and said: 'I have a nice picture of you at home and a nice picture of the beautiful house you have in the country. If I don't get the money for my payroll by this evening, I am going to print both these pictures in the local newspaper. Under your picture it will say "This is the man who is responsible for city employees not being paid" and under the picture of your house it will say "And this is where he lives".' He then put down the phone. The ruse worked and Curley got his money on time.

His view of Tip O'Neill was extremely basic: 'He's a fat bastard.'

SENATOR EUGENE MCCARTHY on being a successful politician: 'It is like being a football coach. You have to be smart enough to understand the game and dumb enough to think it's important.'

WHEN SENATOR Robert Kennedy was standing in the Democratic presidential primaries in 1968 he was due to address a meeting of farmers. He arrived rather early and walked in to the back of the room, where he was unnoticed at first. He overheard some of the farmers grumbling about what a drain it would be on the budget 'if those nine or ten Kennedy children get into the White House'. Announcing his arrival, he then added: 'Yes, I've got ten kids and they all drink milk. Tell me anyone else who is doing that much for the farmer.'

FORMER US PRESIDENT Richard Nixon has always been a controversial figure. On politics he has remarked: 'There is one thing solid and fundamental in politics – the law of change. What's "up" today is "down" tomorrow.'

His advice to young politicians: 'Always remember others may hate you but those who hate you don't win unless you hate them. And then you destroy yourself.'

His maxim for political success: 'To be popular in office, you need an enemy. Reagan had the USSR and Congress. Clinton, as yet, has not found one.'

His thumb-nail assessment of President Boris Yeltsin has yet to be bettered: 'He burns all his candles at both ends and he is compulsive. I give him only slightly more than a 50 per cent chance of success. But he's got guts.'

To an aide: 'Use all the rhetoric, so long as it doesn't cost money.'

And: 'Voters quickly forget what a man says.'

Harry Truman disliked Nixon, calling him 'a no-good lying bastard'. Adding for good measure: 'He can lie out of both sides of his mouth at the same time, and even if he caught himself telling the truth, he'd lie just to keep his hand in.'

Despite a landslide re-election victory Nixon never completed his second term, being forced to resign in disgrace following the Watergate Hearings. Recently, showing that he has a sense of humour, he said: 'I hear that whenever anyone in the White House tells a lie, I get a royalty.'

DURING THE term of office of President Nixon, a Republican Senator wanted Congress to appropriate $600 million to help bring the nation's sewage disposal system up to date. He knew that President Nixon was opposed to the measure and, therefore, he prepared a well-argued and detailed speech on the subject, in which he discussed household effluent and the waste-disposal systems in some detail.

When he finished his address, New Hampshire Senator Norris Cotton approached him and said: 'I never realized until now what you're an expert on, but now I know.' 'What's that, Norris?' asked the senator. Cotton responded tersely: 'Shit.' The senator was nonplussed for a moment and then recovered the situation with his response: 'Norris, can you think of anything more important to be an expert on in the Senate than that?'

FORMER AMERICAN PRESIDENT Gerald Ford was frequently ridiculed in satire shows for his clumsiness. However, occasionally he put his detractors in their place. He once said: 'A bronco is something that kicks and bucks, twists and turns, and very seldom goes in one direction. We have one of those things here in Washington – it's called the Congress.'

Ford served in Congress before achieving his country's highest office. Once when Hubert Humphrey was making a lengthy speech, Ford, who had just entered the chamber, asked his neighbour: 'What follows Humphrey?' And he received the riposte: 'Christmas.'

Humphrey agreed that he was often long-winded remarking to one colleague: 'I can't even clear my throat in less than three minutes.'

NIXON'S VICE-PRESIDENT Spiro Agnew must have sounded somewhat like Leonard Sachs of TV's *The Good Old Days* when he said his opponents in Congress were 'pusillanimous pussyfooters', adding for good measure, 'They are nattering nabobs of negativism.'

IN 1973 beef prices in America were soaring. In order to try to protect the consumer, Congressman Frank Annunzio from Chicago introduced an amendment in committee to freeze the price of beef. Somewhat to his surprise the amendment was passed.

Afterwards he was interviewed by the *Wall Street Journal* and he expressed his pleasure at the successful amendment adding, 'This is a victory for the American people.'

However, as if often the case in politics, his victory was short-lived. Overnight, beef farmers went into action and started lobbying politicians. They were so successful that the next day the committee voted to reconsider Annunzio's amendment and decided to reject it.

The same reporter from the *Wall Street Journal* sought out the Chicago congressman and asked him again for his reaction now that his amendment had been rejected. Rather tersely Annunzio stated: 'The American people got fucked.' The shocked reporter protested: 'I can't use that quote – this is a family newspaper.' Turning to leave, Annunzio snapped: 'In that case, tell them the American *family* got fucked,' and walked off.

AND ON that subject, Mrs Lillian Carter, the mother of former US President Jimmy surprised even the liberal press when she said: 'Sometimes when I look at my children, I say to myself, "Lillian, you should have stayed a virgin."'

THE USE of the insult during an election campaign can backfire, particularly if the public perceive that the gibe is unfair or just downright nasty. Governor Pat Brown of California, when challenged at the polls by Ronald Reagan, ran a series of insulting television adverts that opened with the line 'I am running against an actor . . . and you know who killed Abraham Lincoln, don't you?' This backfired badly and Reagan won the subsequent election by a landslide.

Reagan's more restrained retort to Pat Brown was: 'He is one of those Liberals* who thinks that all the world's problems can be solved by throwing taxpayers' money at them.'

PRESIDENT RONALD REAGAN was known as 'The Great Communicator' due to his consummate skill on television, and also, on Capitol Hill, as 'The Great Persuader' because of his ability to persuade a number of Democrats, who controlled Congress, to agree to his programme. Despite the fact that he never had a majority in the House, Reagan managed to push through most of his manifesto by splitting the opposition.

His popularity was – and is – undoubtedly due to the fact that he comes over on television as 'a nice guy' – someone totally free of malice. However, when he thought the occasion demanded it, he was not afraid to use invective to make his

---

* The word 'liberal' has a different connotation in USA politics to its UK meaning. Reagan was being derogatory. Our equivalent description would be 'left-winger'.

point. Before the collapse of Communism he caused a furore when he referred to the USSR as 'the evil empire'. Liberal opinion was similarly outraged in 1986 when he referred to Iran as 'Murder Incorporated'.

During his presidency Reagan maintained his friendships with the world of showbusiness. Once, at a White House banquet he found himself talking to old friend Bob Hope, a golf fanatic. Hope inquired whether Reagan had any time for golf and asked the President: 'What's your handicap?' Reagan shot back: 'Congress.'

Reagan on former Speaker of the House Tip O'Neill: 'He could be sincere and friendly when he wanted to be, but he could also turn off his charm and friendship like a light-switch and become as blood-thirsty as a piranha.'

On former Secretary of State Alexander Haig: 'He would pound the table and seemed ready to explode. He was insecure. I thought he was seeing shadows in a mirror.'

During the 1984 presidential race, when Reagan was seeking re-election, his opponent Walter Mondale quipped: 'I don't like to attack Ronald Reagan as being too old for the job, but I remember that in his first movie Gabby Hayes got the girl.'

When governor of California, Reagan was faced with a delegation of students who took over his office. Some were barefooted, several were wearing torn T-shirts and when the governor entered the room, no one stood up. The ringleader said to Reagan: 'We want to talk to you but we think it's impossible for you to understand us. You weren't raised in a time of instant communications or satellites and computers, solving problems in seconds. We now live in an age of space travel and journeys to the moon, of jet travel and high speed electronics. You didn't have those things when you were young ...' At this point Reagan interrupted the student spokesman and said: 'No, we didn't have those things when we were your age – we invented them.' Not only did Reagan silence the students, but he let it be known that his only policy would be that they should: 'Obey the rules or get out.'

During his period as President and before the Berlin Wall was pulled down, one of Reagan's favourite stories was of Leonid Brezhnev on his death bed giving advice to his successor Mr Andropov. Raising himself on one arm Brezhnev said: 'Let me give you one piece of advice. When you take over from me, make sure in whatever you do that the Soviet people follow you.' At which point Andropov replied to the dying Brezhnev: 'Don't worry. If they don't follow me, I'll make sure that they follow you.'

In the 1988 American presidential race, answering a journalist's reference to his young age for such high office, Dan Quayle, then candidate for the vice-presidency, pointed out that John Kennedy was of a similar age when he stood for the presidency. This led the Democratic vice-presidential candidate Lloyd Bentsen to say 'I knew President Kennedy and Senator you're no Jack Kennedy.' The insult hurt but it was not until four years later that a Republican politician turned the insult back upon the Democrats. On the opening day of the Republican convention in 1992, Reagan referred to Bill Clinton's claim that he was the new Thomas Jefferson with the barb: 'I knew Thomas Jefferson. He was a friend of mine – and Governor Clinton ain't no Thomas Jefferson.'

Early in his presidency even his opponents were impressed by Reagan's first televised budget speech, in which he used a handful of small change to illustrate the effects of inflation on the value of the dollar. A Democratic rival observed: 'Carter would have emphasized all the wrong words. Ford would have fumbled and dropped the cash. Nixon would have pocketed it.'

On the Democrats' election promises: 'When you hear all of that smoky rhetoric billowing out, take the advice of Bill Clinton – don't inhale.'

Former MP Denis (now Lord) Healey was not impressed

with Reagan's economic record, saying: 'He has done for monetarism what the Boston Strangler did for door-to-door salesmen.'

And the views of veteran Republican Barry Goldwater on the former actor President: 'He can't decide whether he was born in a log cabin or a manger.'

FORMER PRESIDENT George Bush had a vicious line on his Democratic opponent during the 1992 election: 'I consulted with John Major and other leaders on foreign policy issues – Bill Clinton takes advice from Boy George.'

In a similar vein, again on Clinton: 'While I bit the bullet, he bit his nails. His policy can be summed up by a road sign he's probably seen, "slippery when wet". He says he's for one thing and then comes out for another. He's like that on a lot of issues – first one side then the other. He's been spotted in more places than Elvis Presley.'

On Clinton's policies: 'He says he wants to tax the rich, but he defines rich as anyone who has a job. You've heard of the separation of powers. Well Bill Clinton practises a different theory – the power of separations. His government would have the power to separate you from your wallet.'

And returning to his Presley theme: 'Clinton's plan for America really is "Elvis economics" – the country will be checking into the Heartbreak Hotel!'

His comments before polling day on the way the Clinton campaign was conducted could with hindsight be applied to his own performance. He unwisely remarked: 'It reminds me of the old conman's advice to the new kid when he said, "Son, if you're being run out of town, just get in front and make it look like a parade."'

On Andrew Young: 'He is a loose canon on a rolling deck.'

The penchant of a free press to exaggerate bad news is

well-known. Lord Tombs of Rolls-Royce once startled a group of reporters by announcing: 'Gentlemen, I have a problem for you. We have just won a massive order which secures hundreds of jobs. I, therefore, have only good news to announce. You won't have a typeface small enough for the story.' After months of gloomy news reports, just before his failed re-election bid Bush, in a similar vein, remarked: 'When the Berlin Wall fell, I half expected to see a headline "Wall falls, three border guards lose jobs".'

FORMER AMERICAN VICE-PRESIDENT Dan Quayle has long been the butt-end of press criticism and political sniping from the Democrats. However, Quayle, apart from one spelling lapse, has generally confounded his critics. During the early stages of the 1992 presidential election he gave his detractors ammunition by mis-spelling potato as 'potatoe'. This led to howls of derision which Quayle turned back against the Democrats by quipping: 'If Bill Clinton is a moderate, then I am a world-champion speller.'

THOMAS 'TIP' O'NEILL, Speaker of the House of Representatives, was for many years one of America's most colourful public figures. He retired in 1986 having served for 34 years as a member of Congress, ten of those as Speaker – the longest continuous term in the United States.

Commenting on Christian Herter, a former poliician from Massachusetts, he said: 'He was extremely partisan. The rules, as he understood them said "screw the Democrats".'

On John F Kennedy: 'The first time I met Jack Kennedy I couldn't believe this skinny pasty-looking kid was a candidate for anything! He had absolutely no political experience. Although he was a Democrat, looking back I'd say he was only nominally a Democrat. He was a Kennedy, which was more than a family affiliation. It quickly developed into an entire political party. He certainly knew how to charm the ladies and he always made a point of appealing to what he called 'womanpower – the untapped resource'.

On Bobby Kennedy: 'He was a self-important upstart and a know-it-all. Jack Kennedy had not grown up in the school of hard knocks. He was used to people loving him and if somebody said something mean about him and it got back to him, he would wonder why they didn't like him. But with Bobby ... when Bobby hated you, you stayed hated.'

On former Congressman Howard Smith of Virginia: 'A taciturn, arrogant son of a bitch who was no more a Democrat than the man in the moon. As far as he was concerned, the civil war was still going on.'

On former President Lyndon Johnson: 'As a professional politician he had the right idea but he was crude about it. His political style was overwhelming and there was nothing subtle about it.'

And his view of the Kennedy–Johnson relationship: 'The Vice-Presidency is never an easy office to occupy but it rankled Johnson that this young, rich upstart was in the White House while he, who had come up the hard way, was the all-but-forgotten number two man.'

His comments on former presidential hopeful Eugene McCarthy: 'He was a whimsical fellow with a meanness in his heart. He was lazy and a bit of a dreamer. He had the support of all the way-out flaky Liberals in the country.'

On Wayne Hayes, a former congressman: 'He was an excellent orator but had a mean streak and was often abusive to people he didn't agree with. Even when he praised you he did it with a nasty twist. When he resigned from Congress most of us were delighted to see him go.'

O'Neill's view of the American news reporting team of Evans and Novak: 'They ought to be called "Errors and No-facts".'

On politics: 'Power is never given — it is only taken.'

On former President Richard Nixon: 'He was brilliant but he had a quirk in his personality that made him suspicious of everybody — including members of his own cabinet. He was a leery and nervous president.'

On former President Gerald Ford: 'Although he was wrong most of the time, he was decently wrong.'

On former presidential hopeful George McGovern: 'His nomination was a disaster. He never should have been selected as the Democratic candidate but he was chosen by the cast of *Hair*. I was absolutely shocked when the young people in the party picked him as their champion. The party has an occasional suicidal tendency and you didn't need to be a pollster like Harris to see that McGovern was going to get creamed. In the eyes of many Americans, George McGovern was so far to the left he was off the map.'

On former President Jimmy Carter: 'He came in young and vigorous but left a tired man. When it came to the politics of Washington, he never really understood how the system worked — he didn't want to learn about it either. He rode into town like a knight on a white horse, but while the gentleman leading the charge was capable, too many of the troops he brought with him were amateurs. But that didn't prevent them from being arrogant. Too many of his aides — especially his Chief of Staff Hamilton Jordan — came to Washington with a chip on their shoulder and never changed. Those guys came in like a bunch of jerks and went out the same way.'

And warming to his main target, Mr Jordan: 'He is a son of a bitch. As far as he is concerned, the House Speaker is something you bought on sale at Radio Shack. I prefer to call him Hannibal Jerken.'

When O'Neill became Speaker of the United States House of Representatives, a young congressman asked him why he was not being included in the decision making. O'Neill shot back: 'Although I take you seriously, you must remember that when a storm comes along, I don't want to grab on to a young sapling that sways in the wind. In difficult times, I prefer to go with the sturdy old oak.'

And his view on the difference between the two houses in the US Congress: 'Congressmen are the workhorses while senators are the showhorses.'

On political lobbying: 'I believe that public protest is more effective than a silent diplomacy. I am convinced that the squeaky wheel gets the grease.'

And expanding his views on the subject: 'When someone asks me why the Greeks in American always get a hearing for their side, and the Turks can't get anywhere, I will say: "That's because nobody knows a Turk, but everybody knows the people who run all those restaurants." It's the same with the Arab–Israeli conflict. The experts can come up with a dozen reasons to explain why America supports Israel, usually that Israel is the only true democracy in the Middle East or that the Soviet Union used to provide huge arms shipments to Israel's enemies. That might be true enough, but to the average American it often boils down to something more basic – the fact that some of his friends and neighbours happen to be Jewish. The answer is simple. All politics is local.'

Amongst his other comments the following are worthy of note:

'The press, in its cynical way, loves to portray just about every congressional trip as a junket.'

'Money is the mother's milk of politics.'

On the office of President: 'What Jimmy Carter failed to understand is that the American people want a majesterial air in the White House which explains why the Kennedys and the Reagans were far more popular than the Carters and the Lyndon Johnsons – most people prefer a little pomp in their Presidents.'

On former President Ronald Reagan: 'The press saw Lyndon Johnson as crude, Richard Nixon as a liar, Gerald Ford as a bumbler, Jimmy Carter as incompetent, but they were certainly rooting for Ronald Reagan. Reagan has enormous personal appeal and he quickly became a folk hero. He performed so beautifully on the tube that he could sell anything but he has been a rich man's President. He has shown no care or compassion for the poor, but when it comes to giving money to the Pentagon or tax breaks to the wealthy, Reagan has a heart of gold. He is Herbert Hoover with a smile. He is a cheerleader for selfishness.'

Continuing his attack on Reagan, he did concede the former President's strengths: 'In 1986 he started singing that familiar song that those Americans who were out of work could get jobs if they really wanted to. I couldn't believe he was still spouting this nonsense. This was Ronald Reagan at his worst, but later that same day I saw the President at his best. After our first meeting the space shuttle Challenger exploded after take-off and that evening the President went on television. He made a masterly speech and as I listened to him, I had a tear in my eye and a lump in my throat. Ronald Reagan may have lacked some of the management skills that a President needs, but he's the best public speaker ever and in this respect he dwarfs both Roosevelt and Kennedy.'

On the congressmen elected on the coat-tails of President Reagan's popularity: 'They were nothing – just Reagan Robots.'

Getting his own back Reagan commented on Tip O'Neill (a man about the same height as Reagan but considerably larger in girth): 'I like to keep in shape by jogging three times a day around Tip O'Neill.'

A member of the public was not quite as tactful. When he saw O'Neill leaving a plane he buttonholed the Speaker and said: 'Leave the President alone, you fat bastard.'

TELEVISION CAN be deceptive. As Margaret Thatcher once said: 'Selective seeing is believing.' After the United States Congress admitted television cameras, a number of representatives would take advantage of the 'Special Orders' procedure to attack their opponents. This is a part of the day in Congress which is similar to the adjournment debate in the British House of Commons. It is a period at the end of the day's business where any member is entitled to take the floor and to speak for up to an hour (in the British House of Commons it is usually limited to 30 minutes) on any subject of his choosing. On most occasions the House chamber is empty and Special Orders speeches are usually made for consumption back in the constituency. On one occasion Robert Walker a congressman from Pennsylvania used his speech to attack another congressman who he knew had left the building. He attacked his colleague's voting record and generally criticized him. Under the rules of Congress, the television camera was focused only on Walker, so anyone watching TV at home would assume that not only was the House full, but that also the politician being insulted was sitting, inert, just listening to the diatribe. To encourage this perception Walker would pause from time to time as if to give his opponent the chance to reply. The inference drawn by the viewer was that the man being slagged off was actually accepting by his silence the criticism being levelled.

Walker might have got away with this, but for the fact that Tip O'Neill, then House Speaker, was watching the performance from the television monitor in his office. O'Neill called the director of television and told him to pan the cameras around the entire chamber. He did so and the television viewer then saw that the chamber was empty. Walker's tactics, therefore, backfired badly, although he and his fellow Republicans did lodge a complaint against O'Neill for altering the rules of transmission. O'Neill had the last word by publicly rebuking Walker and his colleague, Congressman Gingrich, for attempting to deceive the public.

♠

FORMER CONGRESSMAN John Le Boutillier had a sharp tongue for nearly everyone. Commenting on Harvard University he said: 'The University is filled with hypocritical, bleeding-heart leftists.'

At the time of his election in 1980 Le Boutillier, who was only 27, was the youngest member of Congress but that didn't stop him from insulting some senior US politicians. He referred to President Carter as 'a complete bird-brain', Democratic presidential hopeful George McGovern was dismissed as 'scum', and he called Speaker Tip O'Neill 'big, fat, and out of control – just like the Federal Government'.

He even went to the unusual lengths of campaigning against the Speaker's re-election using the slogan 'Repeal O'Neill'. Despite this O'Neill was comfortably re-elected.

♠

AUTHOR PHILIP STERN caused a furore in 1988 with his book *The Best Congress Money Can Buy*. To attempt to make his point he put a one dollar note inside 509 copies of his book and posted them to all members of Congress.

A few of the dollars were returned with a brief note from the congressmen concerned saying that they could not accept cash; some congressmen kept the money and the book, but Stern was surprised with the letter he received from Jerry Lewis, the Californian Republican representative who returned the dollar note wrapped in toilet paper. In an accompanying letter Lewis wrote: 'Anyone who presumes that people who seek to serve in public affairs can have their principles purchased by one dollar, or one thousand dollars, should look into the mirror and carefully measure their own character.' Senator Jesse Helmes went one better. He kept the dollar

BILL CLINTON ON GEORGE BUSH when challenged as to why he had not answered accusations made by Mr Bush during the 1992 presidential election: 'Why should I interrupt my opponent when he is making a fool of himself?'

and wrote back: 'I don't resent your implication that Congress can be "bought" because I am willing to assume that you have some exceptions in mind and that I am one of the exceptions.'

♠

LEADING REPUBLICAN SENATOR Robert Dole has a sharp turn of phrase. Commenting about the US Congress he has said: 'The first month I was there, I wondered how I ever got in. And ever since I've been wondering how the rest of them got in.'

When Dole ran for his party's presidential nomination against George Bush, some party members were concerned that his virulent attacks on Bush would damage the chances of both men. Answering this criticism Dole snapped: 'I will stop telling the truth about Bush, if he stops telling lies about me.'

After a meeting between three ex-presidents Dole commented: 'At a party a few weeks ago, I saw Carter, Ford and Nixon – See No Evil, Hear No Evil and Evil.'

♠

A MISSISSIPPI CONGRESSMAN, Robert Roberts, was once assailed by a constituent who complained that he took little part in debates in the House of Representatives while other congressmen made many speeches and attracted a lot of national attention. Roberts took his constituent to task, replying: 'When I was a young man, I used to ride a horse and whenever I came to the bank of a stream, I put my ear to the ground and ascertained whether water made a noise. At that place, I always marched in – it was sure to be the shallowest place.' And with that he walked off.

♠

ALTHOUGH MOST politicians are adept at the art of the put-down, sometimes they receive their come-uppance from a most unusual quarter. In 1987 Senator Bill Bradley was having a meal and asked the waiter for more butter. He was duly given an extra pat. Later on he asked the same waiter if he could have yet more butter, to which the waiter replied: 'Sorry, but I've already given you two portions.' Bradley turned upon the waiter and said: 'I don't think you know who I am. I am Bill Bradley the Rhodes scholar, ex-professional basketball player, a world champion, and now United States senator.' Without batting an eyelid the waiter replied: 'Well, perhaps you don't know who I am.' Bradley exploded: 'Well, I don't, who are you?' To which the waiter replied: 'Well, I'm the man who's in charge of the butter,' before disappearing out of the dining-room.

THE OFFICE of vice-president of the United States of America is perhaps the most maligned position in *any* democracy. Franklin D Roosevelt said that the job was 'the spare tyre in the US government'.

Roosevelt's vice-president was John Nance Garner who said that 'a great man may be a vice-president, but he can't be a great vice-president because the office in itself is unimportant'.

President Kennedy summed up why the post can be an unrewarding one: 'The vice-presidency is the worst of both worlds. You don't have any power and the Secret Service is always on your tail.'

Lyndon Johnson had practical experience of the job. He was VP to Kennedy before becoming President himself following Kennedy's assassination. He thought even less of the number two job saying that it wasn't worth 'a pitcher of warm piss'.

Earlier, John Adams, the first US vice-president, said: 'My country has in its wisdom contrived for me the most insignificant office that has ever been conceived by the imagination of man.'

Referring to the vice-president's duty of having to preside over sittings of the senate, Adams continued: 'It is a punishment to have to hear other men talk five hours every day and not be at liberty to talk at all oneself.'

Harry Truman, who was Franklin D Roosevelt's third vice-president, had a similar turn of phrase to Johnson. Being marginally less crude he said of vice-presidents: 'They are about as useful as a cow's fifth teat.'

Roosevelt appeared to share these sentiments. Once, when a tinkling chandelier in the White House disturbed his slumbers, he ordered the staff to remove it. When he was asked what should be done with the offending item he said: 'Take it to the vice-president – he needs something to' keep him awake.'

Walter Mondale, whose challenge for the presidency against Ronald Reagan ended in disaster, had previously served as vice-president. He shared the views previously expressed about the office. He often told the story about a man who lived near Three Mile Island who had been assured by an expert that the area was safe from radioactivity 'because the President had visited the area'. When the man questioned this and asked: 'What makes you think that that proves it is safer' he received the response: 'If it wasn't safe, they would have sent the vice-president.'

A CANDIDATE for a North Carolina constituency called Frank Grist was furious when the local paper wrote an article which concluded: 'Frank Grist is not qualified to be a dog catcher.' On the advice of his lawyer he sent a telegram to the newspaper threatening to sue for libel unless it retracted its comments. The paper duly obliged and in the next edition carried the following: 'Frank Grist is fit to be a dog catcher, but instead of running for that office, he is seeking the post of United States senator.'

🏛️

ONE US CONGRESSMAN received a highly critical letter from a woman in his home town who was upset by the way he had voted. In the course of her missive she said: 'Congressman, even if you were St Peter, because of what you have done, I would not vote for you.' The congressman wrote back explaining the reasons for his vote and added at the end of his letter: 'I note your statement, that even if I were St Peter you wouldn't vote for me. Allow me to point out, however, that if I was St Peter, you couldn't vote for me. You wouldn't be in my district.'

🏛️

TAKING A swipe at education wets, Republican Representative John Ashbrook said: 'A Harvard professor is an educator who thinks that the American eagle has two left wings.'

🏛️

DURING THE 1992 presidential election George Bush called the Democratic team 'a couple of bozos', which lead to the retort from President Clinton: 'All I can say is a bozo makes people laugh and Bush makes people cry ... and America is going to be laughing on election night.'

🏛️

IN THE United States political invective during an election is known as 'negative campaigning'. In America candidates are allowed to advertise on both radio and television and a recent survey revealed that almost 90 per cent of these adverts are 'negative'. Rather than extol the virtues of the candidate who is paying for the advert, it appears that it is more effective to rubbish one's opponent.

My favourite 'negative' ad was one used by an unknown candidate who was fighting an experienced and long-serving incumbent in a state election. The incumbent, predictably, ran a series of ads emphasizing his experience adding that he had 'been serving in the Statehouse a long time' and was 'the voice of experience'.

The response of his challenger was devastating. Against a background shot of someone attempting to slice a golf ball, a voice-over said: 'Do you have an elderly uncle who likes playing golf? You know, he's been playing it for years. He is very experienced at the game. And yet he's just as bad now as when he first started! Well, it's the same over at the Statehouse.'

The challenger won the seat.

THE FORMER United States Senator for Ohio, Stephen Young, once received a letter saying: 'You are a stupid fool for favouring gun control. I am sure you could walk upright under a snake's tail with your hat on and have plenty of headroom.' The constituent also gave his address and telephone number and said: 'I would welcome the opportunity to have intercourse with you.'

Young rose to this insult and replied: 'Sir, I am in receipt of your most insulting letter, and I note your offer in the final paragraph where you welcome the opportunity of me having intercourse with you. No, indeed. You go ahead and have intercourse with yourself.'

Young also said to a local lawyer who insisted on giving him some advice as to how he should vote: 'Don't give me any more of this unsolicited advice. I know it costs nothing, but that is exactly what it's worth.'

Summing up his own philosophy he said: 'Sarcasm is the sour cream of wit.'

4
Order, Order!

FORMER DEPUTY PRIME MINISTER Lord Whitelaw on his own career: 'The Tory Party does not like brains. Thank God I don't have any.'

*

GOVERNMENT MINISTER Anne Widdecombe on Labour's front-bench spokesman Michael Meacher: 'If Dr Spooner were alive, he would call him a shining wit.'

*

TORY BACK-BENCHER on Dennis Skinner: 'It makes good sense to strike whilst the iron is hot – but he strikes when the head is hot.'

*

LORD THOMPSON, a former Labour politician, summed up the view of many journalists when he said: 'The trouble with all politicians is that they over-react to the broadcasters.'

*

LABOUR BACK-BENCH MP Alan Williams on the Conservative government: 'They have walked not on water, but on oil. And after twelve oil-rich years we are in recession. Now, they are trying to walk on hot air.'

*

WELSH NATIONALIST MP Dafydd Wigley on former Labour leader Neil Kinnock 'On constitutional issues we trust him as far as we could drop-kick him.'

*

TORY BACKBENCHER Sir Ivan Lawrence once silenced an opponent with the barb: 'If everything you knew was added to everything I knew, I wouldn't know any more.'

*

FORMER FRENCH PRESIDENT Georges Pompidou gave the following interesting definition: 'A Statesman is a politician who places himself at the service of the nation. A politician is a statesman who places the nation at his service.'

*

FORMER SPEAKER of the US Congress Joe Cannon on the man who loses: 'There is nothing deader than the defeated presidential candidate.'

*

DEFENCE SECRETARY Malcolm Rifkind: 'Scotland needs the Labour Party as much as Sicily needs the Mafia.'

*

FOREIGN OFFICE MINISTER Douglas Hogg on Labour's Gerald Kaufman: 'He is the Obadiah Slope of the House of Commons.'

*

IN A rather gruesome vein Jim Sillars, the former deputy leader of the Scottish Nationalist Party said: 'To get into Downing Street, Neil Kinnock would boil his granny down for glue.'

*

FORMER CHANCELLOR of the Exchequer Nigel Lawson on the break-up of the USSR: 'The disintegration of the collectivized economies of the former Soviet Union was a rare example of an historical experiment testing a theory to destruction.'

*

THE EARL OF CHESTERFIELD who died in 1773 accurately described the behaviour of politicians when he said: 'An injury is much sooner forgotten than an insult.'

*

WHEREAS EDMUND BURKE understated the nature of politicians with his remark: 'I am convinced that we have a degree of delight in the real misfortuncs and pains of others.'

*

LADY ASTOR summed up the appeal of the wealthy: 'The only thing I like about rich people is their money.'

*

POLITICAL OBSERVER Walter Bagehot accurately pointed out: 'One of the great pleasures in life is doing what people say you cannot do.'

His view of do-gooders: 'Nothing is more unpleasant than a virtuous person with a mean mind.'

*

A J BALFOUR on the Conservative Party: 'It is not the principle of the Conservative Party to stab its leaders in the back, but I must confess that it often appears to be a practice.'

*

LORD MELBOURNE said: 'Nobody learns anything from experience – we all do the same thing over and over again.'

*

SHORTLY BEFORE he became Prime Minister in 1937, Neville Chamberlain showed a rare sharp turn of phrase, chiding the Labour Party for 'professing to support the League of Nations with horse, foot and artillery, whereas they really only support it with threats, insults and perorations'.

*

KEN LIVINGSTONE commenting on the bad press he usually receives: 'If I blow my nose the tabloid papers would say I'm trying to spread germ warfare.'

KONRAD ADENAUER, who was the first Chancellor of West Germany, neatly summed up the qualities a politician needs when he said: 'A thick skin is a gift from God.'

Adenauer once put his own doctor in his place. When he was in his eighties he developed a heavy cold which his family thought might be fatal. During his treatment his doctor said: 'I am not a miracle worker you know – I cannot succeed in making you younger,' to which Adenauer snapped: 'I am not asking you to make me younger – I want you to succeed in making me older.'

*

AUTHOR AND Liberal activist G K Chesterton, no doubt with an eye on politicians, said: 'The men who really believe in themselves are all in lunatic asylums.'

On his own philosophy he quipped: 'I believe in getting into hot water – it keeps you clean.'

*

GOUGH WHITLAM, the former Prime Minister of Australia, once got so agitated with an aide that he shouted: 'I do not mind the Liberals, still less do I mind the party calling me a bastard. In some circumstances, I am only doing my job as they do. But I hope that you will not publicly call me a bastard, as some bastards in the caucus have.'

Whitlam was in favour of abortion on demand and during an election rally a heckler continually interrupted his speech with the shout: 'Tell us about your policy on abortion'. Whitlam silenced the heckler with: 'Well, in your case it ought to be retrospective.'

When he was asked to be guest speaker at a banquet given by the Lord Mayor of London in 1974, he opened with: 'I am told, my Lord Mayor, that you were a rowing blue. I was such myself. It is, of course, an extraordinarily apt sport for men in public life – because you can face one way whilst going the other.'

*

PERCEPTIVELY Otto von Bismarck said of politicians: 'When they say they approve of something in principle, it means they haven't the slightest intention of putting it into practice.'

And on speech-making he was equally incisive: 'Many a poor political speech has been saved by throwing in a few lines about patriotism.'

*

I SUSPECT that life would be better if more ministers across the globe heeded the words of Lord Falkland: 'When it is not necessary to make a decision, it is necessary not to make a decision.'

*

SIR ALEC DOUGLAS-HOME, now Lord Home, former Prime Minister: 'There are two problems in my life. The political ones are insoluble, and the economic ones are incomprehensible.'

And Sir Alec on former Labour leader Harold Wilson: 'He is nothing more than a slick salesman of synthetic science.'

*

WIT, WRITER and one-time Member of Parliament Sir Alan Herbert quipped: 'A highbrow is the kind of person who looks at a sausage and thinks of Picasso.'

*

THE LATE Lord Mancroft had a nice line when dealing with a belligerent heckler who was shouting at him. He shouted back: 'A man with your low intelligence should have a voice to match.'

*

WHEN HE was deposed as ruler of Egypt, King Farouk quipped: 'There will soon only be five kings left in the world, the kings of England, diamonds, hearts, spades and clubs.'

*

PRINCE PHILLIP has always spoken his mind and frequently raises a few eyebrows when he expresses his thoughts. On British politicians he said: 'To understand what ministers are sometimes saying, you must buy a gobbledegook dictionary and add an arbitrary ten years to every promise they make.'

*

GERMAN DICTATOR Adolf Hitler had a rather basic view of education: 'Knowledge is ruin to many young men.'
  On political rallies: 'All epoch-making revolutionary events have been produced not by the written, but by the spoken word.'

*

FOREIGN SECRETARY Douglas Hurd on the possibility of a 1992 Liberal–Labour alliance: 'To expect the Liberals to control Labour would be like asking Dad's Army to restrain the Mongol hordes.'

*

WHEN A friend expressed his support Lord Melbourne retorted: 'I don't need fellows to support me when I'm right. I need fellows who support me when I'm wrong.'

*

DEFENCE MINISTER Nicholas Soames on John Major's aims for a classless society: 'This talk is a load of ullage.'
  And Soames on Margaret Thatcher: 'She carried the cult

of the individual much too far and has done us terrible damage in Europe with her fishwife yelling and screaming.'

*

FORMER FOREIGN SECRETARY and now SLD Peer, Lord (David) Owen has accurately summed up most parliamentary advisors: 'A consultant is someone who will take your watch off your wrist – and tell you what time it is.'

*

CHIEF SECRETARY to the Treasury Michael Portillo commenting on Labour's 1992 election plans: 'Their designer Socialism turned out to be a blueprint for losing a record fourth election on the trot.'

His comments on Labour leader John Smith are terse: 'He's a "fudger".'

*

LABOUR MP Giles Radice on Lord Joseph (formerly Sir Keith Joseph MP): 'He is the lamest of lame ducks.'

*

THE COMMENTS by Viscount Morley of Blackburn ought to be written on the tombstone of all dictators: 'You have not converted a man because you have silenced him.'

His observation on democratic politics: 'The choice is constantly between two evils.'

On President Theodore Roosevelt: 'He is a combination of St Paul and St Vitus.'

*

AN ASTUTE comment by Lord Boyd-Orr: 'If people have to choose between freedom and sandwiches, they will take sandwiches.'

*

LORD SALISBURY had little time for the *Daily Mail*: 'A paper by office boys for office boys.'

*

LORD HILL, former politician and chairman of the BBC: 'The point about politicians is that they regard something that is impartial on TV as being biased against them and something that is biased in their favour as being beautifully impartial.'

*

FORMER CABINET MINISTER Jim Prior on Margaret Thatcher's method of settling Cabinet disputes: 'If you disagreed with her, you did not get a fresh examination of the problem. It was fresh faces – she reshuffled the Cabinet.'

*

GIVING ADVICE to a new member, Charles Hill, the former Conservative MP, was scathing of his own government when he advised: 'It does not do to appear clever. Advancement in the Conservative Party is due entirely to alcoholic stupidity.'

*

DURING THE Falklands War Tory MP Robert Adley did not have much time for the BBC, which he called 'General Galtieri's Fifth Column in Britain'.

*

LORD CHALFONT, a former Labour minister, appears to share Mr Adley's concern. His view of the BBC: 'It is a nest of Communists, militants and left-wing agitators of all persuasions.'

*

TORY MP Sir John Wheeler on Labour's Roy Hattersley: 'He reminds me of a 50p piece — two-faced and seven-sided.'

*

LABOUR'S DONALD ANDERSON on Margaret Thatcher: 'She believes she can treat television interviewers just like a Cabinet.'

*

THE IRISH MP John P Curran surprised an opponent when, in response to being told that he spoke rubbish, he said: 'When I can't talk sense, I talk metaphor.'

*

LABOUR MP Lawrence Cunliffe also surprised a few colleagues when he remarked of himself: 'I am in the spring-time of my senility.'

*

LABOUR'S GERALD KAUFMAN on the government's EC policy: 'The Tories do not have a European platform. They have a see-saw.'

*

JUNIOR GOVERNMENT minister Eric Forth on the Labour Party: 'One of the most nauseating sights in the House is the Opposition, with their plans for universal benefits, trying to bribe people with their own money.'

*

A COLLEAGUE commenting on former Tory Prime Minister Sir Anthony Eden: 'The trouble with Anthony is that he is half mad baronet and half beautiful woman.'

Former Labour heavyweight Nye Bevan on Sir Anthony's claim that Britain was invading Egypt (during the Suez War) to strengthen the United Nations: 'Every burglar, of course, could say the same thing. He could argue that he was entering the house in order to train the police. So if Sir Anthony is sincere in what he is saying – and he may be – then he is too stupid to be Prime Minister.'

*

SDP PEER Viscount Chandos commenting on the poll tax: 'If a camel is a horse designed by a committee, the poll tax is a vampire designed by a Cabinet sub-committee. It is mis-conceived, mis-shapen and Mrs Thatcher's.'

*

FORMER LABOUR LEADER Michael Foot on the economy: 'I have no doubt we will get out of the recession some time. When we do, the Prime Minister and others will no doubt tell us it is the greatest miracle since the loaves and fishes.'

*

CHANCELLOR Kenneth Clarke on politics in the 1990s: 'We are into an era of mass media and everything is more belligerent than it was.'

*

FORMER SPEAKER of the House of Representatives 'Tip' O'Neill summed up the attitude of most politicians when he said: 'I am against any deal I am not in on.'

*

LORD ARMSTRONG commenting on the civil service: 'Their job is the orderly management of decline.'

*

WHEN LABOUR'S George Galloway asked fellow Socialist MP Gordon McMaster: 'Why do so many people take an instant

JOHN MAJOR ON JOHN SMITH: 'He has as much likelihood of understanding how the economy works as Donald Duck has of winning *Mastermind*.'

dislike to me?' He was lost for words when McMaster replied: 'Oh, it saves so much time.'

*

TORY JOHN BIFFEN on his former leader Edward Heath: 'He has a glacial personality.'

*

PENNSYLVANIA SENATOR Boies Penrose on political etiquette: 'In politics it is all right to apologize to an individual. But never apologize to a mob. The first is gracious; the second is cowardly.'

*

HOME SECRETARY Michael Howard on Neil Kinnock: 'He has the consistency of the chameleon and the wisdom of the weathercock.'

*

PRESIDENT GRANT of the USA on Senator Charles Sumner: 'The reason the senator doesn't believe in the Bible is because he didn't write it himself.'

*

LADY OLGA MAITLAND, newly elected to the House in 1992, surprised some of her colleagues when she said: 'I don't want to become a circus act – I don't want to be another Edwina Currie.'

*

MISSOURI CONGRESSMAN Richard Gephardt did not endear himself to the combatants when during a debate on the Middle East crisis he commented: 'I don't see why the Arabs and Jews can't sit down and settle this like good Christians.'

*

FORMER PRESIDENT William Howard Taft was perceptive in his observation: 'Enthusiasm for a cause sometimes warps judgement.'

*

FORMER LEADER of the Soviet Union Nikita Khrushchev once described his political philosophy thus: 'When you are skinning your customers, you should leave some skin on to grow so that you can skin them again.'

His view of how to react to others: 'I have no use for the party of the Gospels and their advice "If someone slaps you, just turn the other cheek." I intend to show that if anyone slapped us on our cheek, they would get their head kicked off.'

*

COMPLAINTS ABOUT German politicians in peacetime are not a new phenomenon on the Tory benches. In 1925 our then Foreign Office Minister Austen Chamberlain said: 'The German government is like a nagging woman. It must have the last word.'

*

KING GEORGE V on Foreign Secretary Sir Samuel Hoare: 'No more coals to Newcastle, no more Hoares to Paris.'

*

LORD DENNING, former Master of the Rolls, has said: 'Two reasonable persons could perfectly reasonably come to opposite conclusions on the same set of facts without forfeiting their right to be regarded as reasonable.'

*

OF ONE CONGRESSMAN from South Carolina named Rivers an opponent quipped: 'I never knew that Mendel Rivers drank until I saw him sober.'

5
Who Said That?

OVER THE years many quips, insults and witticisms are remembered whilst their originators have been forgotten. Here are some from both sides of the Atlantic.

*

A WET TORY overheard commenting on his former leader, Margaret Thatcher: 'I owe a lot to her – my ulcers, nausea, and headaches.'

*

TOLD AT Westminster: 'When Neil Kinnock visited a zoo it took four hours to persuade. him to leave. They had just finished feeding the animals, so he stopped to make a speech.'

*

WHEN ONE Labour back-bencher said that John Prescott was a 'self-made man' his colleague replied: 'That is a big argument against do-it-yourself.'

*

ON THE late Randolph Churchill: 'A chain drinker.'

*

'MANY AN MP who thinks he has an open mind, in reality only has a vacant one.'

*

ON MARGARET THATCHER: 'She objects to ideas only when others have them.'

*

'SOME POLITICIANS are like fish. They see the bait but not the hook.'

*

'MANY PEERS look busy but they are only confused.'

*

'IN POLITICS a man must learn to rise above principle.'

*

SOMETIMES GRAFFITI artists have the last word over politicians. At the time of the negotiations on the Anglo-Irish agreement a Democratic Unionist supporter daubed 'Ulster says no' on a wall. Later some wag wrote underneath 'But the man from Del Monte says yes.' A few weeks later another graffiti artist topped even that with the line 'And he's an orangeman.'

*

POLITICIANS IN difficulty rarely get sympathy. Most colleagues follow the maxim: 'Everyone pushes a falling fence.'

*

'MANY MINISTERS only have a clear conscience because they have a poor memory.'

*

WHEN ONE MP commented: 'I thought Ian Paisley just made a good speech', his colleague replied: 'Oh, it was superfluous! Simply superfluous. He ought to have it published posthumously – and the sooner the better.'

*

ONE MP who was troubled was advised by his Whip that all he had to do was to look his misfortunes right in the face and laugh at them. He replied: 'I wouldn't dare. Neither my wife nor my mother-in-law has a sense of humour.'

*

'JIMMY CARTER as President is like Truman Capote marrying

Dolly Parton. The job is just too big for him.'

*

ON PRESIDENT Bill Clinton: 'He's the Karaoke Kid – he'd sing anything to get elected.'

*

COMMENT ON a junior minister: 'He works like a horse – and everybody appears to ride him.'

*

WHEN A visiting constituent asked why Capitol Hill had a rotunda, one of the guides is alleged to have replied: 'It's so the statesmen find it easier to run round in circles.'

*

THE STORY is told of three Socialists, Tony Blair, Roy Hattersley and John Prescott who, whilst on holiday abroad, made a wager. They decided to bet who could remain the longest in a mountain cabin with a skunk. Tony Blair managed it for just a minute. Roy Hattersley beat him easily, managing to stay in the room some two minutes. Then John Prescott went in and the door was bolted behind him. After only 15 seconds, John and Roy heard this frantic scratching noise from inside the cabin. They decided to open the door to see what was happening and the skunk ran out.

*

ON A speech by Norman (now Lord) Tebbit: 'His remarks were well balanced – they were all rotten.'

*

WHEN A back-bench MP referring to a problem in his constituency said: 'No news is good news' his Whip intervened, echoing the words of Nicholas Bentley: 'No journalist is even better.'

*

ON A particular Cabinet minister: 'He is the only politician who can dig himself into a hole – and out again within seven days.'

*

TONY BLAIR says he will be Prime Minister one day – I think one day will be long enough.'

*

ONE HAS to admire the candid response of the failed candidate for Congress who, on his election defeat being announced, said: 'This is democracy. The people have spoken – the bastards.'

*

LAST YEAR a young lad was paying his first visit to the Palace of Westminster and was eagerly waiting with his parents to meet his MP, when the Division Bell sounded causing a number of ushers and police officers to hurry about their business. 'What's that bell for?' his father said to his mother. The boy innocently piped in: 'I think one of them has escaped.'

*

A YOUNG MP in conversation with some of his colleagues said: 'Every married man should try to forget his mistakes.' His Whip agreed, adding: 'There is no use in two people remembering the same thing.'

*

A TORY back-bencher is fond of telling a story about the MP

and his party Whip who both arrived in heaven at the same time and how the Whip was given a lavish suite of rooms with the use of a swimming pool, whilst the MP was given a small bedsitter with just a plank of wood for a bed. When the MP complained bitterly about this unreasonable treatment, St Peter said: 'I know how you feel, but we have got thousands of MPs up here; this is our first Whip.'

*

DURING 1976 the then Labour government had both a relatively new Leader of the House, Michael Foot, and also Chief Whip, Michael Cocks. During the summer of that year they made a number of misjudgements due to their inexperience which led to some Labour MPs referring to them as 'Foot-in-it' and 'Cock-up'.

*

HEARING NEIL KINNOCK explain Labour's election programme in 1992, a Conservative back-bencher surprised his audience when his first comments were: 'Neil Kinnock's arguments are sound ... but only sound.'

*

ONE MP claims that 'The food is so bad in the Members' Tea Room that they should have Andrew's Liver Salts on tap.'

*

WHEN AN MP in the Members' Dining Room held his fork in the air with a piece of meat on it and remarked: 'Is this tripe?' a government Whip sitting nearby was heard to remark: 'To which end of the fork are you referring?'

*

ON JOHN MAJOR: 'If he is not too careful, he'll carry this Citizen's Charter idea too far. Public services and living conditions will improve so much that we're going to run out of humble beginnings for our future Prime Ministers.'

*

ON LABOUR'S Gerald Kaufman MP: 'He started by trying to move mountains, but ended up by merely throwing dirt.'

*

WHEN A back-bench MP proffered the advice: 'Never bite the hand that feeds you,' he was interrupted by a Whip who said: 'Oh, I don't know. The mosquito doesn't do too badly out of that philosophy.'

*

'NOTHING IS more frequent than an MP going for an occasional drink.'

*

ON A junior minister: 'He is like a piece of blotting paper – he soaks it all in but unfortunately gets it backwards.'

*

THE WHIP'S advice to a young bachelor MP: 'To marry a woman for her beauty is like buying a house for its paint.'

*

COMMENT BY a newly-married member: 'The only books I have seen with unhappy endings are cheque books.'

*

ON BEING criticized for not flattening a Labour back-bencher during a debate, one minister loftily replied: 'Eagles do not catch flies.'

*

A WHINGING back-bencher was silenced with the comment: 'If you have the right to complain when there is nothing to complain about – then you are living in a democracy.'

*

ON TONY BENN: 'No foresight – no hindsight – just left-sight.'

*

INSULTS ARE their most effective when used to put down someone who has an unusually high opinion of himself, or is fond of boasting about the attributes, achievements or success of members of his family. On one occasion an MP was boring his friend with boasts about his father's longevity. 'My father was a remarkable man. He lived to be 109 years of age,' the politician boasted. He was withered by the response: 'I have never known a person who lived to that age be remembered for anything else.'

*

SOMETIMES INSULTS gain a momentum of their own, particularly when they emanate as a result of a rumour. Car manufacturers Skoda have long been the butt-end of comedians' jokes about the quality of workmanship of their cars. At first the company appeared happy to go along with the jokes, but they changed their mind when the wisecracks started to get out of hand.

Some members of the House of Commons Motor Club have not been slow to join the attack on Skoda cars and the following barbs have been heard in the corridors of Westminster:

'What do you call a convertible Skoda? A rubbish skip.'

'How do you double the value of a Skoda? Fill it with petrol.'

'What is the difference between a golf ball and a Skoda? You can drive a golf ball 50 yards.'

'What is the difference between a Skoda and a sheep? You feel slightly less embarrassed being seen getting out of the back of a sheep.' (This remark came from a West Country MP.)

'Why do Skoda cars have heated rear windows? To keep your hands warm when pushing.'

And according to one MP, a Skoda owner who went into a garage and inquired: 'Could I have a petrol cap for a Skoda?' received the reply: 'That sounds like a fair swap to me.'

In addition to their problems with insults getting out of hand, production at Skoda's Mlada Bolesav plant came to a halt towards the end of 1989. Most of the workers were prisoners who vanished after Czechoslovakia's new president, Vaclav Havel, announced an amnesty!

*

THE EAST MIDLANDS Electricity Board ran a series of adverts featuring a near-naked Brian Clough. Recently an MP involved in advertising was asked if he thought it was a good campaign. His response sounded enthusiastic: 'As the aim of most advertisements is to make you remember the name of the advertiser, then this must be judged as a good advertising campaign. I think of nothing else. I am still trying to work out why the revolting spectacle of some overweight loud-mouthed semi-clad socialist should encourage me to support the Electricity Board.'

*

ON ALICE MAHON MP: 'Kiss her under the mistletoe? I wouldn't kiss her under an anaesthetic.'

*

ECHOING THE comments of John Sparrow, an MP was over-heard remarking on an opponent: 'If only he'd wash his neck, I'd wring it.'

*

WHEN A back-bencher was bragging that his wife always did what he wanted and added: 'I've got her eating out of my hand,' his Whip cautioned: 'In that case, it's a good idea to count your fingers.'

*

'MY SECRETARY'S speed for typing is nothing special, but she can talk 80 words a minute.'

*

WHEN AN MP asked his Whip for an extra day off just before the Christmas recess, he received the response: 'If you want to miss tomorrow's vote, kindly note the piece of mistletoe hanging from the tail of my jacket.'

*

COMMENTING ABOUT the weather in Blackpool during the Labour Party Conference, an MP was heard to say: 'The weather was so bad here last week, the tide didn't come in – it came down.'

*

ON ONE particular Labour MP: 'She is so ugly I bet when she was born, her mother fed her by catapult.'

*

READING IN the Tea Room just after the 1992 election, a new MP commented: 'Isn't it amazing? Every time I breathe in and out, someone dies somewhere in the world.' This caused his Whip to inquire: 'Have you ever thought of using a mouthwash?'

*

THE BRITISH are often said to be 'good sports' and that in business dealings we 'play cricket'. An American politician visiting Westminster, using a similar analogy, but pointing out that he did business another way, said: 'Play ball with me and I'll stick the bat up your arse.'

*

A STUDENT who had taken a summer job working as a researcher to an MP was asked late one Friday afternoon to undertake a job which would have taken a couple of hours. 'I can't do that,' the student replied, 'because today is POETS day.' 'POETS day?' inquired the member. 'What do you mean?' 'Piss Off Early Tomorrow's Saturday,' the surprised MP was told.

*

LORD SAMUEL said: 'A friend in need is a friend to be avoided,' which was rather more elegant than a Tory back-bencher who recently said: 'A friend in need is a bleeding nuisance.'•

*

MOST POLITICIANS at some stage of their career have practised dontopedology – which, to use the vernacular, means 'to put one's foot in it'. Like the Labour Cabinet minister who, when offered a cigar by King George VI, said: 'No thank you – I only smoke on special occasions.'

A similar *faux pas* was committed by Lady Caroline Douglas-Home when she said of her father Sir Alec, who was criticized for being out of touch when he assumed the leadership of the Conservative Party: 'I cannot see how anyone can say he is out of touch. He is used to dealing with workers on his estate.'

*

FOLLOWING THE tabloid coverage of the difficulties in Fergie's marriage and her relationship with two Americans, this below-the-belt remark was overheard on the Terrace of the Commons: 'I always used to think it was the Duke of York who had 10,000 men ...'

*

ON LABOUR'S Gordon Brown: 'He's lost his marble.'

*

ON LABOUR'S Peter Mandelson: 'A whale's tongue is found to contain 8 per cent of the oil in its system. In Mr Mandelson, the proportion is considerably higher.'

*

'A FUNNY thing happened to Harriet Harman last week – she opened her mouth and a foot fell out.'

*

ON JOHN PRESCOTT: 'He keeps behaving like an untipped waiter.'

*

ON TERESA GORMAN MP: 'She is not so much overdressed as just wrapped up in herself.'

*

WHEN ONE MP said to a colleague, 'Your wife is outspoken,' he received the reply: 'By whom?'

*

COMMENT ON Mildred Gordon MP: 'The trouble with her is that so many square meals have made her round.'

*

ON DOUGLAS HOGG MP: 'His candour is insolence in black tie.'

*

ON ROY HATTERSLEY: 'He won't leave any footprints on the sands of time because he is too busy covering his tracks.'

*

ON DAVID WINNICK MP: 'He has a finger in every pot and a hand in nothing.'

*

ON A minister: 'He promises too much too soon and accomplishes too little too late.'

*

ON RON DAVIES MP: 'The reason he is so easily rattled is because he has a screw loose.'

*

ON IAN PAISLEY MP: 'Well at least he has achieved a sort of balance – his narrow mind goes with his broad tongue.'

*

ON TONY BLAIR: 'He has nothing to say but you have to listen a long time to find that out.'

*

ON TONY BENN MP: 'He can trace his ancestors back a long way – and he's been descending ever since.'

*

ON DALE CAMPBELL-SAVOURS MP: 'Any mediocrity can gain attention through slander.'

*

TWO MPS were discussing a particular government Whip. The

first remarked: 'He's capable of assassinating anyone.' This drew the response from his colleague: 'Assassinating, no – poisoning, yes.'

*

'PADDY ASHDOWN is not thinking about this particular issue – he is merely re-arranging his prejudices.'

*

ON SIMON HUGHES: 'It is necessary that he has a long nose since he cannot see beyond it.'

*

'BEING ATTACKED by Gerald Kaufman is rather like being hit by a large cream cake. You are not injured – but rather sickened.'

*

COMMENT ON Denzil Davies MP: 'It only takes one drink to get him going – but he's not sure whether it's the tenth or eleventh.'

*

'NEVER TRUST a man who speaks well of everybody.'

*

WHEN ONE MP lost a considerable amount of money at Lloyds, his pair remarked: 'His house is covered with more mortgages than paint.'

*

ON THE speech of an MP: 'I keep reading between the lies.'

*

A WOMAN who thought rather a lot of herself was at the piano

JAMES PRIOR ON MARGARET THATCHER: 'She was Boadicea, hammering away at those wicked people seeking to carry out policies alien to her trusted beliefs and nature.'

entertaining her guests. At one point she stopped, turned around and said to the local MP who was guest of honour: 'I hear that you love music.' 'Yes,' the MP replied. 'But never mind, just keep on playing.'

*

ON CHRIS MULLIN MP: 'The original red herring.'

*

IN THE early days after the death of Robert Maxwell MPs were still speculating as to the case of his death. In the brief period before the massive fraud on his own pension funds was discovered, many still thought Maxwell may have been murdered. When the scale of the fraud and wrongdoing became clear, most MPs regarded the death as suicide. During this period one MP wondered whether Maxwell had regretted his actions and perhaps sought forgiveness from God. This led to the riposte: 'Don't make me laugh – right to the end he probably thought the Good Samaritan should have been arrested for loitering.'

Also overheard on former MP Robert Maxwell: 'He was as straight as a concertina. In the end he was a man who had too many double-crosses to bear.'

*

ON MARTIN REDMOND MP (seen taking a book into the House of Commons library): 'He must have finished colouring it.'

*

TORY BACK-BENCHER on Britain's European Commissioner Leon Brittan: 'He always looks as if he has got a stocking mask over his head.'

*

ON **ANDREW BENNETT** MP: 'He thinks hirsuteness is a substitute for astuteness.'

*

ON **BILL CASH** MP: 'I suppose he is self-sufficient – rather like an ostrich carrying his own bucket of sand round with him.'

*

ON **TEDDY TAYLOR** MP: 'He is so intense, he doesn't burn a candle even at one end.'

*

ON **JAMES PAWSEY** MP: 'He's got so many children, he used to pay income tax on his child benefit.'

*

ON **DENNIS SKINNER** MP: 'He is but a fraction of the working-class intake in the House – and a vulgar fraction at that.'

*

THE TORY candidate Mitchell Hepburn addressing a crowd at a farm meeting, spoke from the rear of a manure spreader. He opened his remarks with the quip: 'This is the first time in my life that I have spoken from a Tory platform.' At this point a heckler yelled back: 'Someone throw the machine in high gear – it's never had a bigger load on.'

*

COMMENT ON Ronnie Campbell MP: 'If, during a disagreement with him, it ever comes to a choice of weapons – choose grammar.'

*

ON **FORMER** President Gerald Ford being interviewed on

camera: 'He looks like the man in a science fiction movie who is the first to see the Creature.'

*

'CYRIL SMITH is as attractive to look at as Loyd Grossman is to listen to.'

*

ON CLARE SHORT MP: 'She's the thinking woman's Cyril Smith.'

*

ON A female Labour MP: 'She ought to have a sign saying "please let the bus go first" on her face.'

*

ON FORMER MP Dr Alan Glynn: 'I wouldn't say he was old, but on his birthday if you just put the cake ingredients in a pan and light the candles, the cake cooks itself.'

*

ON ROBERT MACLENNAN MP: 'He ought to bore a hole in himself and let the sap run out.'

*

ON THE Reverend William McCrea MP: 'I wish he would confine his activities to preaching – then I'd only have to listen to him on a Sunday.'

*

DURING THE 1992 general election one Tory back-bencher was surprised when the door was answered by a vicar wearing his dog collar. He decided to try to solicit the reverend's vote when the holy man asked: 'Tell me, do you ever take alcoholic drink?' Showing himself to be up to the measure of the occasion, the politician replied: 'Excuse me, is that an inquiry or an invitation?'

*

ON PAUL BOATENG MP: 'The only tense he uses in speaking is pretence.'

*

ON MALCOLM BRUCE MP: 'He has hidden talents – well hidden.'

*

THE GOSSIP at Westminster in 1993 is that Neil Kinnock is set to become an author. Rumour has it that he is about to translate the *Kama Sutra* into Welsh. His critics say he is well-qualified to do so having been in every position himself except Number 10.

*

ON EDDIE LOYDEN MP: 'He looks like an Egyptian mummy without the bandages.'

*

ON PADDY ASHDOWN: 'The only big thing about him is his opinion of himself.'

*

ON GWYNETH DUNWOODY MP: 'She had such a pretty chin, she decided to add two more.'

*

ON MRS MILDRED GORDON MP: 'Her clothes look rather good, considering the shape they're on.'

*

ON PETER HAIN MP: 'The reason he always walks with his nose in the air is to avoid smelling himself.'

*

ON MARION ROE MP: 'I am not sure if that's a new hairdo, or she's just walked through a wind tunnel.'

*

ON AUSTIN MITCHELL MP: 'It would take him five minutes to boil a three-minute egg.'

*

ON NEIL KINNOCK MP: 'They put brighter heads than his on matchsticks.'

*

ON TONY BANKS MP: 'I don't think he can swim. He surely couldn't keep his mouth closed for long enough.'

*

ON FRANK DOBSON: 'The trouble with him is that he's forgotten but not gone.'

*

ON TONY BLAIR: 'Not so much a man of promise, but a man of promises.'

*

ON FORMER LABOUR Cabinet minister Barbara Castle: 'The only time she had a figure was when she had mumps.'

*

COMMENT ON Lady Thatcher: 'When she dies, *everyone* will rest in peace.'

*

ON NORMAN (NOW LORD) TEBBIT: 'He has a concrete mind – permanently set.'

*

ON MARIA FYFE MP: 'When she speaks, she makes the same noise as bath water running down the plughole – only I can understand the bath water.'

*

ON DENNIS TURNER MP: 'Singers run in his family – and so they should.'

*

ON FORMER LIBERAL MP Cyril Smith: 'He could make a fortune helping people lose weight. One look at him would make anyone lose their appetite.'

*

ON GEOFFREY DICKENS MP: 'He ought to close his mouth before someone puts an apple in it.'

*

ON RICHARD BODY MP: 'I am not sure if that's dandruff on his shoulders or sawdust leaking out of his ears.'

*

ON LORD TEBBIT: 'He should put some variety in his life and find something new to hate.'

*

ON FORMER MP Dave Nellist: 'The only way he'll ever get polish is to drink it.'

*

ON IAN MCCARTNEY MP: 'He's so short that if he pulled his socks up, he'd be blindfolded.'

Again on Ian McCartney: 'He is so small that you can't even wipe your feet on him.'

*

ON NIGEL GRIFFITHS MP: 'If he wore stilts he'd still be a midget.'

*

ON GEOFFREY DICKENS MP: 'He always enters a room voice first.'

*

ON HARRIET HARMAN MP: 'She is a good example of why God created man first – so he would have a chance to say something.'

*

ON A former government minister: 'If there was an Olympics for bad judgement, she would break all records.'

*

ON ALICE MAHON MP: 'Her speeches are like medicine – hard to swallow.'

*

ON CLARE SHORT MP: 'I'd like to buy her something to put round her neck – a rope.'

*

ON IAN BRUCE MP: 'He ought to use his head – it's the little things that count.'

*

ON ANN CLYWD MP: 'I liked her when we first met, but she talked me out of it.'

*

ON TONY BANKS MP: 'He ought to be a member of the Parole Board. He never lets anyone finish a sentence.'

*

ON NEIL KINNOCK MP: 'He could make a fortune by hiring himself out to fill hot-air balloons.'

*

A LABOUR COLLEAGUE on Tony Benn: 'He has had more roads to Damascus than a Syrian long-distance lorry driver.'

*

ON FORMER Tory Party Chairman Chris Patten: 'He doesn't need to wear jewellery. He already has enough rings under his eyes.'

*

ON PADDY ASHDOWN MP: 'There are two sides to every question – and he always takes both.'

*

ON A speech by Geoffrey Dickens MP: 'I've seen better arguments in a bowl of alphabet soup.'

*

ON ANN WIDDECOMBE MP: 'If she went to a mindreader, she'd only be charged half price.'

*

WHEN A particularly pompous MP said to a waiter: 'Who do you think you're talking to?' he was amazed with the reply: 'I don't know sir, how many guesses do I get?'

*

ON DR JOHN BLACKBURN MP: 'I hope he lives to be as old as his jokes.'

*

TORY COMMENTING on Tony Banks MP: 'He must have a large brain to hold so much ignorance.'

*

ON FORMER MP Nigel Lawson: 'He has always been conceited. When he was young he joined the Navy so the world could see him.'

*

ON FORMER MP Dave Nellist: 'People like him don't grow on trees – they swing on them.'

*

ON FORMER MP (now a peer) Bob Mellish: 'He makes Alf Garnett look like Mother Theresa.'

*

TORY BACK-BENCHER on former EU President Jacques Delors: 'He is the Arthur Scargill of Europe.'

*

TORY MP John Carlisle has a keen interest in the activities of South Africa. His knowledge and expertise on the country frequently infuriate a number of Labour left-wingers who feel that he is too pro-Pretoria. During one debate as he rose to speak, a Labour back-bencher was heard to shout: 'Here is the Member for Johannesburg North.'

*

LABOUR MP commenting on Social Security Minister Roger Evans: 'He is a cross between Bertie Wooster and Billy Bunter.'

*

WHEN A junior health minister commented: 'Scientists are right when they say we are what we eat,' a government Whip muttered from the back of the meeting: 'Nuts must be a commoner diet than we had all thought.'

*

ONE BACK-BENCH MP accurately described the feelings of many Londoners when he quipped: 'It's a pity that the only people who know how to run the country are too busy driving taxi cabs.'

*

A COMMENT on a speech by Labour MP Dr Jeremy Bray: 'Watching him perform in the House is like having a ringside seat at a chapel of rest.'

*

'WHAT HAS 36 legs and 4 teeth?' 'The front row at a Fabian meeting.'

*

WHEN THE actress Glenda Jackson was first elected to the House as Labour MP for Hampstead and Highgate, a Tory back-bencher was heard to remark: 'Ah yes. I am reminded of the words of Kipling.' His colleagues thought he was about to gush forth a compliment when he added: 'A rag and a bone and a hank of hair.'

Also on Miss Jackson: 'If she's just turned 50, it must have been a U-turn.'

*

ON A female Tory MP: 'She has a face that could launch a thousand dredgers.'

*

ON A Labour back-bencher: 'He is as good as his word – and his word is no good.'

*

AN INSULT can, of course, be a gesture rather than words but to be really effective it needs to be rather more subtle than the two-fingered variety. Once, when having a drink at a bar in a snooty golf club, an MP was approached by an extremely pompous official who told him that it was against club rules 'not to wear a tie in the clubhouse, no matter how hot it was'.

At this and without demurring the MP who was sporting an open-neck shirt, promptly left the clubroom and went to his car. He returned five minutes later sure enough wearing his tie – but no shirt!

*

MP COMMENTING on a tabloid journalist: 'He picks up more dirt with the telephone than most people do with a vacuum cleaner.'

*

A YOUNG back-bencher was informing his colleagues of his forthcoming matrimonial intentions and said: 'It was love at first sight.' To which his Whip replied: 'In that case you should have taken a second look.'

*

AFTER A particularly pompous Tory MP had been holding forth in the Tea Room about the world's current financial problems, he was silenced with the barb: 'How is it that you know so much about banking, economics and money and yet have so little of it?'

*

MP DISCUSSING his own marriage: 'Of course my wife and I are compatible – we both love to fight.'

*

AT A reception an MP's wife admitted: 'When my husband speaks in public I tremble.' Which led the husband to confess: 'And when my wife speaks *in private I* tremble.'

*

A RELATIVELY new MP was talking in the Smoking Room and bemoaning the fact that his recent speeches were not as good as the occasions when he addressed the House during his first year in Parliament. 'I just don't think my recent speeches are as good as my earlier ones,' he said. This drew the reply from a government Whip: 'Don't be silly. Your speeches are the same as they ever were. It's just your taste that's improved.'

*

CAUGHT IN a downpour a drenched MP complained to the policeman on duty in New Palace Yard: 'Is there anything worse than an afternoon in London when it's raining cats and dogs?' 'Yes,' replied the police officer. 'An afternoon of hailing cabs.'

*

I CANNOT vouch for the authenticity of this story. When the

Spanish Prime Minister visited Britain immediately after Spain had joined the EC, he was asked by an MP in the welcoming delegation what Spain's most popular sport was. 'Bullfighting,' said the Spanish Prime Minister. The MP looked concerned. 'I always thought that was revolting,' he said. The Prime Minister retorted: 'No, that's our second most popular pastime.'

*

'NO MATTER how low in value the pound may fall, it will never fall as low as some people will stoop to get it.'

*

'WHEN A politician says he has a clear conscience, it often means that he has a bad memory.'

*

'YOU CAN tell when it's summer. It's easy. That's when a Scotsman throws his Christmas tree away.'

*

AN MP reading a newspaper in the Tea Room observed: 'It says here that it takes five years for a tree to produce nuts.' This led a colleague to respond: 'Except in the case of a family tree.'

*

'A CEMETERY is a place filled with people who thought that the world couldn't get along without them.'

*

WHEN HEARING that the left-wing TV critic Melvyn Bragg had said that he always made a practice of 'pausing' before finishing a novel, one MP gibed: 'It's a pity he doesn't pause before beginning one.'

*

'THE REASON new ideas die quickly in some back-benchers' heads is because they cannot stand solitary confinement.'

*

COMMENT BY a government Whip: 'When some MPs think they are arguing with a fool, the problem usually is that the other man is doing the same.'

*

ONE BACK-BENCHER'S comment on a Whip: 'He always thinks twice before he says nothing.'

*

ON ROBIN COOK MP: 'He has made a fool of himself – and that is an improvement.'

And in a similar vein: 'He speaks straight from the shoulder. It is a pity that it is not a little higher up.'

*

ON HEARING a lengthy speech by Austin Mitchell MP, a back-bencher was overheard to remark: 'He seems to think that for a speech to be immortal, it needs to be eternal.'

*

'A NUMBER of politicians only look like giants because they are surrounded by dwarfs.'

*

'HER GREY hair is a sign of age – not wisdom.'

*

'SOME PEOPLE make the mistake of thinking that when a bore leaves the room, someone important has come in.'

*

'HE'S NOT only a bachelor – he is the son of a bachelor.'

*

ON MILDRED GORDON MP: 'She looks like a model ... for a duffel bag.'

*

ON DENNIS TURNER MP: 'He started singing late in life – and didn't stop soon enough.'

*

OF GEORGE FOULKES MP: 'He has nothing to hide because he has nothing to show.'

*

ON NORMAN (NOW LORD) TEBBIT: 'He has such a sharp tongue that he often cuts his own throat.'

*

ON TAM DALYELL MP: 'He often acts like he has a tiger in the tank, but the problem is there is a donkey at the wheel.'

*

'SOME WOMEN do not want to marry political go-getters. They are looking for already gotters.'

*

AND AN MP's advice on world travel: 'In an undeveloped country, don't drink the water. In a developed country – don't breathe the air.'

*

MP TO colleague: 'My doctor says he doesn't believe in

unnecessary surgery – he won't operate unless he really needs the money.'

*

MP TO journalist: 'Do not talk to me about averages. If a man stands with his right foot in an oven and his left foot in a freezer, some statisticians would say that, on average, he is comfortable.'

*

'YOU ALWAYS know when you meet a pessimist. Instead of shaking his hands, he shakes his head.'

*

'IF YOU cannot think of any way to flatter a woman, tell her that she's the kind who can't be flattered.'

*

ON BEING asked why there had never been any women in the government Whips' office, a Whip replied: 'Whips need to be able to trust each other completely – and men can because they know the exact degree of dishonesty they are entitled to expect from each other.'

*

SENIOR TORY MP: 'Roast beef has made England what it is today.' Labour MP (overhearing the comment): 'In that case, eat your vegetables.'

*

MANY A junior minister has denied being a 'yes man' on the basis that when his boss said no, he said no.

*

ON A female MP: 'I won't say she's a gossip, but when the phone rings she reaches for a chair.'

*

'OF COURSE she is a senior politician – she has ceased to grow vertically and now grows horizontally.'

*

A COMMENT on Sydney Chapman MP: 'Yes, he is an optimist – even his old suit has its shiny side.'

*

OVERHEARD OF a politician: 'He was so used to exaggerating that he could not tell the truth without lying.'

*

'ONE NICE thing about egotists is that they do not talk about other people.'

*

'MOST WOMEN seem to have six ages: baby, child, young miss, young woman, young woman, young woman.'

*

'THE BEST service a former minister can render to his country is to turn in his tongue along with his red box and mothball his opinions.'

*

'POLITICIANS VERY often take more time to tell a story than it took for it to happen.'

*

'THESE DAYS society is willing to spend £50,000 to provide a school bus to take the children right to the door so they don't have to walk. Then the local authority has to find a further £200,000 for a gym so the kids can get some exercise.'

*

'THE TROUBLE with most people is that their repartee is what they think of after they have become a departee.'

*

'THE TEST of good manners is being able to put up with bad ones.'

*

'A CONFERENCE is the gathering of people who alone can do nothing, but together can decide that nothing can be done.'

*

'I LIKE long walks – especially when they are taken by people who annoy me.'

*

'THE PROBLEM with those of "artistic temperament" is that so many of them have the temperament without the art.'

*

ON SEEING the Chancellor of the Exchequer entering the House of Commons: 'Here comes Kenneth Clarke, with his hands in his own pockets for a change.'

*

'THE MORE I see of mankind, the more I like my dog.'

*

'SHE HAS nothing to say, but takes a long time saying it.'

*

'HAVING A chip on one's shoulder is usually proof of wood higher up.'

*

WHEN SOMEONE complained of losing his 'train of thought', he was met with the riposte: 'I wouldn't worry if I were you. It's like one of British Rail's trains – it has a certain capacity but is running empty.'

*

'HIS OPEN mind should be closed for repairs.'

*

'TWO RATS will make peace over a carcass.'

*

'SHE WORKS eight hours and sleeps eight hours. The trouble is, it is the same eight hours.'

*

'POLITICIANS ARE like boats – they each make the loudest noise when they're in a fog.'

*

'THE REASON old men refer to the good old days is that they always look better than they were. The reason they are good is because they are not here.'

*

OF A particularly narrow-minded Conservative MP: 'She was so narrow-minded she could see through a keyhole with two eyes.'

*

'A MOB has many heads but no brains.'

*

OVERHEARD AT a meeting of the All-Party Jazz Group: 'What do you call a dog with wings?' 'Linda McCartney.'

*

'HE MAY have an open mind, but a mind that is always open lets in a lot of nonsense.'

*

'LABOUR'S TAX proposals are so exorbitant that they are now clearly the party of capital punishment.'

*

COMMENT BY a government Whip: 'Any man who says he can read a woman like a book is probably illiterate.'

*

'THE AVERAGE temperature in a Commons committee room is 70°. That is 50° in the winter and 90° in the summer.'

*

COMMENT ON an SLD politician: 'He doesn't listen to his conscience because he won't take advice from a total stranger.'

*

AFTER YET another airport delay, a colleague accurately summed up air travel with the gibe: 'An airport is where you go to waste in waiting the time that you are going to save by flying.'

*

'A POLITICIAN knows how the other half ought to live.'

*

'TO ERR is human but to blame the mistake on someone else is the talent of a statesman.'

*

ON A debate on equal pay: 'Women are getting men's wages now – but on reflection, they always were.'

*

OF A Scottish MP: 'He was so silent he was always worth listening to.'

*

ON ARCHIE HAMILTON MP: 'He is so tall that he stands on a chair to brush his teeth.'

*

'BEFORE I start my speech, I'd like to say something.'

*

COMMENT ON the Conservative Party: 'They live by the golden rule: he who has the gold makes the rules.'

*

'BRITAIN'S TABLOID newspapers would all go bankrupt if everyone obeyed the ten commandments.'

*

'IN HIS house antiques are merely the furniture that's been paid for.'

*

WHEN A new MP asked his Whip, 'How do I stand for having next Thursday night off?' he received the reply: 'You don't stand – you grovel.'

*

ON ONE particular government Whip: 'He's the kind of person who throws a drowning man both ends of the rope.'

*

A BACK-BENCHER was overheard saying: 'You can tell we're in a serious recession. Even the people who never pay have stopped buying.'

*

ON A back-bench female MP: 'She has a face that would fade flowers.'

*

COMMENT BY a Labour back-bencher: 'Why are all the windows sealed at Liberal headquarters? To keep all the fairies from flying out.'

*

ON MARGARET THATCHER: 'I have a soft spot for her – there is a swamp at the bottom of my garden.'

*

A COMMENT overheard by a working-class Labour MP on the new Labour leader Tony Blair: 'Of course he's a friend of the working man – and he would rather be his friend than be one.'

*

FOLLOWING THE appointment of some surprising names as life peers a few years ago, the story was told of an MP who was woken by his wife with the comment: 'John, wake up, there are thieves in the house.' Waking from his slumber the MP replied: 'Nonsense my dear – in the Lords, yes, but in the House never!'

*

WHEN TWO back-benchers were talking about a decline in the standards of English in our schools, an education minister passing their table interrupted the conversation and added: 'I agree, a preposition is a very bad word to end a sentence with,' and walked off.

*

'A GOOD politician is one who has prejudices enough to suit the needs of all his constituents.'

*

THE BACK-BENCH MP who said, 'Many wise words are spoken in jest' was interrupted by a colleague who added, 'Yes, but not as many as the number of foolish words spoken in earnest.'

*

AFTER EXPLAINING his opponent's policy, which he described as 'idiotic', an MP told a public meeting: 'Anyone who supports such a scheme is an idiot.' He then asked the question: 'I think we would like to know – are there any idiots in the room? If so, please stand up.' After a pause one man near the back of the hall stood up. 'Why do you consider yourself an idiot?' asked the MP. The reply came: 'I don't, but I hate to see you standing all alone.'

*

AS A joke a colleague sent to a Jewish MP a photograph of a pig. He received back a photograph of his Jewish friend with the note: 'Thanks for your photo; it's only fair that I send you one of me.'

*

ONE SPANISH politician who was being chased by the press for a quote quipped: 'The closed mouth swallows no flies.'

*

'YOU CAN tell when an MP is middle-aged – his narrow waist and broad mind change places.'

*

WHIP TO new back-bencher: 'Marriage is like a violin – after the beautiful music is over, the strings are still attached.'

*

GOVERNMENT WHIP on another politician: 'The bigger the head, the easier it is to fill the shoes.'

*

'THE TROUBLE with wearing a halo is that if it falls a few inches, it can become a noose around the neck.'

*

'HE'S AN MP who has a bright future behind him.'

*

'YOU ARE about as much use as a ribless umbrella.'

*

'THE LABOUR PARTY are fond of sports. One of their favourite amusements is running Britain down.'

*

A BACK-BENCH MP was talking to colleagues and observed: 'We are the law-makers of Britain. We are the instruments of Britain's destiny.' His Whip interjected: 'But mainly wind instruments.'

*

'THE JUNIOR MINISTER who claims to run things in his department can only be referring to the messages, the errands, and making the tea.'

*

ON TONY BLAIR: 'He is unusual all right – his teeth are real, but his tongue is false.'

*

'THERE IS still a belief among some old Conservative knights of the shires that to be uncomfortable is to be virtuous.'

*

AFTER A discussion about a Jeffrey Archer novel an MP was overheard to remark: 'I disagree. The most imaginative fiction being written today is most people's income tax returns.'

*

'A BORE is someone who opens his mouth and puts his feats in it.'

*

OF COURSE, not all insults are verbal in nature. I remember a dispute arising between an MP and a farmer over the boundary between two pieces of land. The MP wrote a letter threatening court action against the farmer unless he removed his fence which was on the MP's land.

The farmer returned the letter with a note saying: 'This is what I think of your letter.' It did not trake the MP long to realize that the letter had been smeared with cow dung.

*

JUST AFTER the Second World War, in view of the Italians'

lack of enthusiasm for fighting, it was said at Westminster that the Italian flag should be 'a white cross on a white background'.

*

DURING THE 1990 Gulf conflict following Iraq's decision to invade Kuwait many British MPs were surprised by the lack of support shown by Britain's European partners towards the efforts of the allied troops. This led to the gibe at Westminster: 'What is the difference between a piece of buttered toast and the rest of Europe?' To which the response was: 'You can make soldiers out of a piece of toast.'

*

MORE RECENTLY, just after the conclusion of the Gulf War, one MP observed that Saddam Hussein and Sarah Brightman now had something in common: 'They've both been screwed by phantoms.'

*

GENERALLY THE bitchiness lasts far longer than the hostilities. Months after we had pulled out of the Gulf I heard the question being asked at Westminster: 'What is the difference between an Iraqi soldier and a pilchard?' The answer was given: 'One is oily and greasy with big bulging eyes – the other is a fish.'

*

AND THE final word on politicians: 'If you ever see a politician who pleases everybody, he will be neither sitting on the left, nor standing on the right. He will be lying flat and there will be a lot of flowers around him.'

GLOSSARY

Insult and invective are far more effective if delivered in a polished and sophisticated manner. Anyone can trade in vulgarities and such abuse is rarely impressive. Unpleasant four-letter words can be heard in the tap-room bar of any public house most nights of the week. They merely reveal the perpetrator to be of limited vocabulary as well as limited intelligence. Because words are weapons, most politicians appreciate that it is the choice of the words used that gives acid-tongued repartee *style*.

What follows is a number of less obvious and obscure words many of which have graced the invective of politicians through the ages. Long may they continue to do so.

ANABIOSIS 'A revival after an apparent death.' An ideal word to use against an opponent who has just woken from his slumbers.

APORIA 'An obviously insincere protestation.' For example, a politician saying he is lost for words.

BAH 'An exclamation of contempt or of impatience.' (Used by Charles Dickens in *A Christmas Carol*, 1843: 'bah', 'humbug' were words frequently uttered by Scrooge.)

BARBARIAN 'An uncultured, uncivilized and uncouth person, especially one who is brutal.' The word appears to come from ancient Greek and was used as a term for anyone who could not be understood, presumably because he didn't speak Greek.

BARMECIDE 'An insincere person who promises but does not deliver.'

BASKET CASE 'Helpless or prone.' The expression appears to have arisen in military circles to describe people who had been injured physically and were suffering from shell shock. More recently, it has been used by politicians mainly in America to describe the economies of other countries when weak (i.e. flat on their back). 'President Gorbachev realized he was the head of an economic basket case' was the view of former US President Ronald Reagan.

BATTOLOGY 'The repeated reiteration of the same words.' Most politicians are experts in this!

BAVARDAGE 'Idle, empty or foolish talk.'

BERK 'A fool or idiot but in origin meaning something rather worse.' The term is Cockney rhyming slang with 'Berk' being an abbreviation of Berkshire Hunt, a term which rhymes with the ancient obscenity for the female vagina. (An alternative in Cockney is Berkeley Hunt – which also has the same meaning as Berk.)

BIMBO 'A young and promiscuous woman, usually a stupid one.' Definitely a woman of easy virtue, but usually younger than the man. The word probably derives from the Italian 'bambino' which means baby.

BLACKGUARD (pronounced **BLAGGARD**) 'Someone without principle; a scoundrel.' The word appears to date from the sixteenth century and has rather fallen into disuse of late. In widespread use in Britain in the early part of the twentieth century but little used now.

BLIGHTER 'A contemptible person, a parasite.' This word is of British origin, presumably from the word 'blight', the implication being that the person so described is rather like a disease. The word dates from the nineteenth century.

BONKERS 'Someone who is insane or crazy with a hint of eccentricity.' The word is British and first appeared in the 1920s when it was mainly used to refer to someone who was 'light-headed'.

BUFFOON 'A clownish half-wit.' The word appears to have originated in Italy where the word 'buffare' means 'to puff'. Frequently used by the late British comedian Tony Hancock but not in general use today.

BUM 'A tramp or idler.' Not in polite use in Britain, but in the United States President Reagan, before the collapse of the USSR, referred to the Polish military government as 'a bunch of lousy bums'.

CACOPHEMISM 'A harsh expression used in place of a milder one.' The opposite of euphemism (e.g. to refer to a gentleman of the press as a hack instead of a journalist).

CAD 'A jumped-up person who is rather vulgar and lacking in principle.' Cad is an abbreviation of the word 'caddie' meaning an errand boy. Has imputations of the British class system implying that the person is rather lowly bred with higher pretensions. The British comedy actor Terry-Thomas was usually cast in this role in many of his movies. Lord Curzon regarded F E Smith as one.

CHARLEY 'A stupid person, an idiot.' Considering the popularity of this disparaging word, it is surprising the number of parents who still have a preference for the boys' name 'Charles', which is frequently abbreviated to this (albeit with a different spelling).

CHISELLER 'Someone who borrows or begs something, usually of relatively small value, with no intention of returning it.' The word is Scottish in origin but appears to have grown in popularity with its crossing of the Atlantic, being in regular use in the United States. So much so that many Americans assume that it is an Americanism.

CLODHOPPER 'A stupid person, especially a slow-witted farmer.' Originally the word probably merely meant someone who 'hopped over clods', but the sense of ungainly stupidity soon gained ground. Agriculture ministers these days are far too sensitive to ever use this about anyone in the farming community.

CRONY 'A close friend or partner in crime.' In politics the term has the implication of someone who has obtained power through friendship rather than ability.

CRYPTO 'Someone who conceals their true beliefs.' Used in the late 1980s by Margaret Thatcher when referring to the then leader of the Labour Party, Neil Kinnock, calling him a 'crypto-Communist'.

CURMUDGEON 'A bad-tempered person, someone who is grisly or grumpy.' The word originated in Britain in the sixteenth century and has now fallen into disuse.

DRIVEL 'Childish, stupid, meaningless nonsense.' The word actually means spittle but has been applied to 'rubbish or nonsense' since about the fourteenth century. A favourite word of former Tory MP Sir Gerald Nabarro.

DYKE 'A lesbian, especially an aggressive masculine one.' A disparaging word, the history of which is uncertain. It may be a shortening of the word 'hermaphrodite'. It has been around since the 1920s.

EMPHOTERIC 'Acting both ways.'

ENDOMORPH 'A short fat person.' An extremely impressive form of insult as very few people will know what it means.

ESURIENT 'A greedy disposition or voracious character.'

EUNUCH 'Literally, a man without testicles, but used to refer to any man who is a weakling.'

FABULIST 'A rather nice euphemism for liar.' Thus it would be quite in order for one MP to refer to another as being 'a well-known fabulist'.

FACINOROUS 'Atrociously wicked.'

FAIRY 'A gay man.' This usage appears to be American in origin, and dates from the latter part of the eighteenth century.

FOGEY 'A person with outdated and old-fashioned ideas, usually someone who is elderly but not necessarily so.' The word dates from the late eighteenth century.

GALOOT 'A clumsy loutish idiot; a showy dimwit' (naval slang).

GLABROUS 'Something that has a surface free from hair;

smooth skinned.' A rather ingenious way of insulting Gerald Kaufman would be to refer to him as one of the century's most glabrous politicians.

GREASEBALL   Originally slang for 'a Greek or Spanish person with thick black hair.' The word appears to have originated in the 1930s. More recently, it has been used to describe any person with an unctuous manner.

HARRIDAN   'A nasty old woman.' A word that appears to have originated from France, the word 'haridelle' meaning a worn-out horse.

HEBETATE   'To grow stupid or dull.' (the noun is hebetude).

HOITY-TOITY   'An arrogant or pretentious person, who is something of a show-off.' The word appears to have originated in the seventeenth century from the obsolete word 'hoit', which meant to romp. Alternative to 'snobby' or 'stuck-up'.

ITHYPHALLIC   Originally a Greek word; 'lewd, indecent, obscene.'

JACKANAPES   'A conceited, impertinent person.' The word has been in use for centuries – certainly since the fourteenth century – but not in popular use in Britain at present.

JACTATION   'Bragging or boasting.' Can also mean 'a false claim or boast.'

KIBOSH   'To terminate, stop, spoil or ruin something.' The word appears to have originated in the nineteenth century and is probably from the Gaelic 'kie bias', which means 'a cap of death', presumably referring to the black cap put on by a judge before sentencing someone to death. The word has also been used to mean 'nonsense'.

KRAUT A slang word for 'a German person' with a hint of insult about it. An abbreviation of 'sauerkraut', the word was popularized during the two World Wars (a sort of culinary insult).

LICKSPITTLE 'An abject sycophant.' The word is almost obsolete today, although it is frequently used by Labour back-bencher Tony Banks, generally to describe any loyal government back-bencher.

LIMACEOUS 'Slug-like, or in connection with slugs.'

LIPPITUDE 'A sore or bleary-eyed condition.'

LUG 'A stupid ham-fisted person.' The word is American in origin and appears to have developed as a form of insult this century. It may derive from 'lugworm', or perhaps even from the verb 'lug' which means 'to drag or pull along' (which is presumably where the word luggage originated).

LUPINE 'Fierce and wolf-like or having the characteristics of a wolf.'

MACROLOGY 'A long and tiresome speech.' It could be said that Austin Mitchell MP is one of Britain's leading mac-rologists.

MEGAPOD 'Having large feet.'

MILKSOP 'A weak effeminate person.' The word has rather fallen into disuse this century, but as an insult, the word has been around since the middle of the thirteenth century. A milksop was originally nothing more than a piece of bread soaked with milk, but it soon came to be used to refer to someone who appeared to be something of a weakling, a sissy.

MOLIMINOUS 'Of great importance or consequence; momentous.'

MUGWUMP 'Someone who is independent politically, usually a Republican who decides not to support his party's candidate.' An American word not in use in Britain. It is applied derisively to maverick politicians ('a man with his mug on one side of the fence and his wump on the other').

MUSH 'Sentimental and soppy nonsense.' The word appears to have originally been a slang description of porridge, but was used to criticize meaningless speech from about the mid-nineteenth century.

MUSSITATION '*Sotto voce* grumbling.'

NEFANDOUS 'Unspeakable,' usually associated with villainy or wickedness.

NERD (also spelt **NURD**) This means 'a stupid person; a loser, particularly one who is socially unacceptable.' The word seems to be of quite recent origin, first being used by American students in the 1960s.

NESCIENCE 'Ignorance or lack of knowledge.'

NIP Slang for a 'measure of alcoholic drink'; also, insulting word for 'a Japanese person'. In its latter context it appears to have been invented by Warner Brothers. In 1944 a cartoon film was released entitled *Bugs Bunny Nips the Nips*. The abbreviation of the word 'nipponese' was undoubtedly part of the American war effort following the Japanese attack on Pearl Harbor. The insult has stuck.

OLIGOPHRENIA 'Mental retardation; feeble-mindedness.'

OTIOSE 'Serving no useful purpose; lazy.' (The word can also mean 'leisurely'.)

PALOOKA 'An inferior or inept person.' Mainly in use in America. Used by the boxing fraternity to mean a punch drunk has-been of a boxer.

PETTIFOGGER 'An unscrupulous, tricky person.' The word appears to have originated in the sixteenth century and has generally been an insult used to refer to a lawyer who would undertake any bad case and argue it to the bitter end. The obsolete English word 'fogger' meant someone who deceived.

PIPSQUEAK 'Someone who is insignificant.' American admiral Ernest King said of President Truman: 'He was nothing more than a pipsqueak haberdasher.' The word originated in the early part of the twentieth century.

PLEBEIAN 'Low or common.' The word is from the Latin 'plebeius' meaning belonging to the common people or 'plebs'.

POPINJAY 'Someone who is conceited without reason, a fop.' The word has been around since the early fourteenth century. The word 'popinjay' was originally used to describe a parrot and hence its insulting use refers to someone who repeats words without really understanding what they mean.

PUDENDUM 'The genitals, usually of a woman.' One MP was overheard recently calling someone 'a stupid pudendum'. (I can't see that catching on down at the local working men's club.)

QUAQUAVERSAL 'Pointing or facing in every direction.'

QUIDNUNC 'A gossip.' Someone who wants to know everything that is going on.

REBARBATIVE 'Off-putting, repulsive or daunting.'

RESIPISCENCE 'Wisdom derived from experience; recognizing one's own errors; seeing reason.'

RODOMONTADE 'Bluster, empty boasting; arrogant ranting; braggadocio.'

RUGOSE 'Having, or being lined with, wrinkles.'

RUSTIC 'A simple-minded country dweller.' Someone without breeding and with poor speech. The term has been used as an insult since about the sixteenth century and comes from the Latin 'rusticus'.

SATRAP 'A petty tyrant, a ruler with despotic powers.'

SCALAWAG 'A rascal; someone without principles.' The word originated in the United States and was first applied to describe those born in the South but who remained faithful to the North during the Civil War.

SLUBBERDEGULLION 'A dirty wretched slob.' The word originated in the seventeenth century as a term of contempt, but has fallen into disuse.

STEATOPYGOUS 'Excessively fat in the hips or fat-buttocked.'

SUCCEDANEUM 'A substitute provided when the real thing is not available.'

TEMULENCY 'Intoxication; drunkenness.'

TERGIVERSATE 'To desert a cause; to change from one opinion to another repeatedly; to equivocate; to become a renegade.' It could be said many political policymakers tergiversate over their manifesto.

THEOMANIA 'Religious insanity; a psychopathic condition in which the sufferer believes that he is God.' Some opponents might argue that David Icke was a borderline case.

TREMULOUS 'Gellatinous; shaking like a jelly.'

ULTRACREPIDARIAN 'Giving an opinion beyond one's knowledge; overstepping the mark; presumptuousness; going too far.'

VARLET 'A rascal or lowly scoundrel.'

VECORDIOUS 'Obsessive or senseless.' The word is used to refer to folly rather than mental insanity.

VELLICATE A verb: 'to twitch, or move convulsively.'

VIRAGO 'A quarrelsome, bad-tempered woman, an amazonian.'

WHIPPERSNAPPER 'A young pushy upstart.'

XENOMANIA 'An obsessive mania for foreign customs, institutions and traditions.' Some MPs would say the British Foreign Office is xenomanic.

YEMELESS 'Careless or negligent.'

Index